Baseball Bafflers 2

THE SECOND INNING

To those

who hate to read

but love baseball.

Baseball Bafflers 2
THE SECOND INNING

*Quizzes, Trivia, Other Ballpark
Challenges, and the Strangest Moments
in Baseball History*

EDITED BY "SLAMMIN'" SAM WEISER

BLACK DOG
& LEVENTHAL
PUBLISHERS
NEW YORK

Published by
Black Dog & Leventhal Publishers, Inc.
151 West 19th Street
New York, NY 10011

Distributed by
Workman Publishing Company
708 Broadway
New York, NY 10003

Designed by Martin Lubin Graphic Design

Printed in the United States of America

h g f e d c b

ISBN: 1-57912-234-5

Library of Congress Cataloging-in-Publication Data
Baseball bafflers 2 : the second inning : quizzes, trivia, other
ballpark challenges and the strangest moments in baseball history /
edited by "Slammin" Sam Weiser.
    p.   cm.
Includes index.
ISBN 1-57912-234-5
1. Baseball–Miscellanea.   I. Title: Baseball bafflers two.   II.
Weiser, Sam, 1989-
GV873 .B244 2002
796.357–dc21
                        2002016478

CONTENTS

Baseball's Funniest Moments

OFFBEAT HUMOR

At times, the brand of humor exhibited in baseball is rather offbeat. The wit can be clever, cruel, self-deprecating, wry, almost philosophical, and even a bit baffling. No other game is as rich in humor as baseball. To paraphrase an interesting theory of writer George Plimpton, in sports, the smaller the size of the ball, the better that sport is in terms of possessing interesting and humorous quotes and stories.

To support his theory, Plimpton pointed out that there are many golf and baseball anecdotes; some football and basketball anecdotes; and, he added whimsically, absolutely none about beach balls.

Aside from the fact that there are no great Ping-Pong stories, his theory seems sound.

A HEADS-UP PLAY

A batter hits a long fly ball that bounces off the center-field fence, strikes the outfielder on the head, and bounces into the stands. The umpire awards the batter a ground-rule double.

Is the ruling a good one?

The umpire is right when he rules that a "bounding" fair ball that is deflected by a player into the stands in fair territory is a double. Once a fly ball hits the fence, it is considered to be a "bounding" ball, not a ball "in flight," and cannot be ruled a home run. A ball "in flight" — that is, a fair fly ball that is deflected by a player into the stands in fair territory — is a home run.

The Expos' Andre Dawson, in a 1977 game at Montreal's Olympic Stadium, rocketed

Is it "bounding" or "in flight"?

a long fly ball to center field that bounded off the wall, struck Dodger outfielder Rick Monday on the head, and bounced into the stands.

Dawson got a double, Monday a headache.

OFF-THE-FENCE INSIDE-THE-PARK HOMER

A batter hits a line drive that bounces out of the glove of the left fielder and flies over the fence. The umpire rules the hit a double.

Is he right?

The umpire, in this case, is wrong and should be overruled. When an umpire miscalls a book rule, another arbiter may reverse his call. This hit should be declared a home run. In the next example, one umpire actually did overrule another one.

In a 1953 game between the Cardinals and the host Braves, Milwaukee's Bill Bruton hit a fly ball that deflected off left fielder Enos Slaughter's glove and bounced over the fence. One umpire called the hit a double; another arbiter reversed the call and awarded the batter a home run.

The second umpire's decision, based upon the rule that a fair fly ball "in flight" that is deflected by a fielder into the stands in fair territory is a home run, was the correct one. Bruton was awarded a game-winning home run.

WHO IS THAT MASKED MAN?

The teams are tied, 3-3, in the bottom half of the 12th inning.

The Giant pitcher, who is in a groove, is mowing down batter after batter. He continues until he gets to the potential second out. The batter lifts a foul fly behind the plate. The Giant catcher quickly discards his mask and circles under the ball. But he steps into his upturned mask and tumbles to the ground as the ball falls to earth untouched.

The catcher has made a physical mistake on the play. But he has committed a mental error, too.

What was the mental mistake?

On a foul pop the catcher should never relieve himself of his mask until he knows the direction of the ball. Then he should flip the mask in the opposite direction.

Such a mistake cost the Giants the 1924 World Series. With the seventh game, against the host

"Look where you're going!"

Senators, tied 3-3 in the 12th inning, Giant pitcher Jack Bentley was in a groove. But with one out in the inning, the Giants let the game get away. The Senators' Muddy Ruel, who had had only one hit in seven games, lifted a harmless foul behind the plate. Hank Gowdy, the Giant catcher, stepped into his discarded mask and fell to the ground. Ruel took advantage of his second chance by doubling to left field. Earl McNeely, the next hitter, bounced a ball to third, but it struck a pebble and ricocheted over Freddie Lindtrom's head for the game-winning and Series-winning hit.

Bentley should have been out of the inning in one-two-three style. Instead, he was the loser in the decisive game of the World Series.

WHAT'S THE SCORE?

A fast-racing outfielder appears to catch a looper hit into center field by the home-team's slugger, but the umpire rules that the speedster trapped the ball after it touched the grass.

The hometown fans, who are furious with the call, hurl objects, such as fruit and bottles, onto the field. Some of the missiles hit two of the umpires. When appeals to the fans, by way of the public address system, fail to quiet the angry spectators, it is evident that something drastic has to be done.

What drastic action do the umpires take?

The umpires, when unable to quiet rioting fans who pose a danger to participants and spectators alike, must rule a forfeit — in this case, to the visiting team. The final score of a forfeit is 9-0. The award-winning team receives one run for every inning of a regulation game.

The Giants of 1949 picked up this type of forfeit when the fans at Connie Mack Stadium in Philadelphia could not be calmed down after an umpire ruled that Phillie center fielder Richie Ashburn had trapped a ball.

Ashburn was one of the greatest defensive center fielders of all time. The Phillie fans, we can suppose, thought that Ashburn could catch any ball that came near him.

THE WAYWARD BALL

A famous player drags a bunt down the first-base line. The pitcher fields the ball and lunges to tag him. But the pitcher loses control of the ball, and it rolls inside the shirt of the runner.

Now, seeing he is in control of the ball, the runner circles the bases while the infielders, in a state of confusion, don't know whether they should chase him or tackle him.

Does the run count?

No, the run doesn't count. When the ball becomes the possession of the runner, he is limited to the base to which he is advancing. In this instance, the runner has to return to first base.

In 1933, Rabbit Maranville, reaching the end of a distinguished Hall-of-Fame career, laid down such a bunt and circled the bases while Dodger pitcher Van Lingle Mungo chased him indecisively from first to home.

The play caused some indecision on the umpires' part, too, and sent them scurrying to the rule book for a verdict on the play.

One base.

WINFIELD GETS THE BIRD

A Yankee outfielder, playing against the host Blue Jays, is warming up between innings. Suddenly a seagull lands on the grass, just a short distance away.

Not knowing the bird is wounded, he impulsively throws at it,

believing that he does not have a chance of hitting it. But the bird, which doesn't move, is killed by the thrown ball.

What is the outfielder's punishment, if any?

Canadians have a fondness for seagulls. So, first, the legal authorities arrest the outfielder. Then the player posts a $500 bond and faces a cruelty-to-animals charge.

Dave Winfield, believe it or not, is the one who faced that charge in Toronto. He suffered a lot of bad publicity before he finally was absolved of the offense.

After that, he limited his putouts to runners, not grounded flyers.

THROWING BEHIND THE RUNNER

Trick plays can be "tricky." Take the catcher's pick-off move, for example.

A Mariner catcher was trying to contain the Royals' base runner, who was on first base. What the catcher decided to do was to look at the pitcher, as though he were throwing to the moundsman, and to throw to first base instead. The first time he attempted his trick move, his first baseman was daydreaming. The catcher's throw sailed past the unsuspecting first baseman and rolled into the right-field corner while the runner scored.

How could the catcher have prevented this unfortunate set of circumstances from taking place?

He should have informed his first baseman in advance, and he would have avoided the disastrous consequences.

Choo-Choo Coleman, catcher for the 1962 Mets, tried to hold the Dodgers' speedster Maury Wills close by using that play. Coleman actually executed the play well. The throw was hard and accurate. There was only one problem: the Mets had a first baseman by the name of Marv Throneberry.

The "Marvelous One" was daydreaming, and he caught the throw right on his forehead. The ball glanced off his head and rolled between the right and center fielders. Wills laughed all the way around the bases.

The moral is, the catcher can look the wrong way, but the first baseman can't.

"Playing first base is such fun!"

KICK BALL

The lead-off batter for the Cubs in a late-season game in Philadelphia bunts toward the right side, but as he breaks out of the batter's box, he accidentally kicks the ball up the first-base line. By the time the pitcher fields the ball and throws to the first baseman, the runner has crossed the bag.

Does he get an infield hit or is he out for interference?

The runner is out when his fair ball touches him before touching a fielder.

In an Indian-A's game in Cleveland, Bert Campaneris, the lead-off batter, stepped into the batter's box as the umpire set himself up behind the plate. As the pitcher went into his windup, the umpire in the field, seeing that his partner behind the plate didn't have his mask on, called "Time." The pitch came anyway, and Campaneris proceeded to push a bunt towards first before running into the rolling ball.

Ordinarily the batter would be called out, but in this instance, the time out preceded the play. So the umpire called the offering no pitch and started the game all over again.

LITTLE LEAGUE PLAY

Some plays that work on a lower level of baseball simply don't work at the Major League level — or at least they shouldn't work. Still, with the right ingredients, anything goes. For example, on May 12, 1998, the Pittsburgh Pirates were playing the Colorado Rockies. Kirt Manwaring laced a ball into right field for an apparent single. Pittsburgh right fielder Jose Guillen came up with the ball quickly and rifled it to first base. Embarrassingly, Manwaring was gunned out. Later, he likened the experience to the feeling you get in a dream where you run as hard as you can, but you don't move at all.

The play worked because of four factors. First, Manwaring, a catcher, is slow-footed. Second, the ball got to Guillen in a hurry.

Third, Guillen fielded the ball quickly, charging in to make the play. Finally, Guillen's arm resembles Roberto Clemente's — it's that good.

MORE EMBARRASSMENT

In 1993, Tom Candiotti was on the mound for the Los Angeles Dodgers when a runner took off for second, attempting a steal. Mike Piazza, who was a rookie catcher that year, came up gunning the ball. The throw was on line, but it never reached second because it struck Candiotti in his derriere.

The knuckleball pitcher later said, "I couldn't help but laugh at that one. I've dodged line drives before, but never a throw from a catcher."

HIT YOUR CUTOFF MAN

When Dave Winfield was with the San Diego Padres, he once went through a bad stretch of games in which he had difficulty hitting his cutoff man.

Shortly after a workout focusing on hitting cutoffs, Winfield had a chance to snap out of his defensive woes. On a hard-hit single to the outfield, Winfield quickly and smoothly came up with the ball in shallow center field.

Darrell Thomas lined himself up with Winfield to take the throw. But he saw that Winfield was very close to the infield, and Thomas knew the strong-armed outfielder would not need him for a relay throw. So, Thomas ducked and spun around to watch the play at the plate.

Meanwhile, Winfield's throw came in hard, low and right on target for the relay man. The ball hit Thomas directly on his backside, much like the Candiotti scenario.

After the game Winfield joked, "I finally hit the cutoff man."

A MICKEY MANTLE TALE

Longtime Detroit Tiger announcer Ernie Harwell recalled what had to be one of the longest singles in the history of the game. He said, "I saw Mickey Mantle hit a ball that bounced into the center-field bleachers at Yankee Stadium. He hit it with the bases loaded in an extra-inning game.

"At first, they gave him a ground-rule double, then they looked it up and could only award him a single." According to the rule book, the batter is awarded a single because it only took a single to drive in the run from third. The only exception to this rule is a game-winning home run. In that situation, they do not take away the homer even if a lesser hit would have won the game (as was the case with Mantle).

"HIDDEN" BALL PLAY

On July 1, 1998, the Chicago White Sox were playing the Houston Astros when, in a weird variation on the old "hidden" ball play, an umpire, not a player, "hid" the ball. Doug Henry was on the mound for Houston, and the Sox had Ray Durham on third.

Atlanta Braves coach Pat Corrales picks up the play-by-play from there: "It looked like the pitch was a sinker, and it hit the ground and bounced up. The ball got by the catcher and went in the umpire's [front] pocket and got buried there.

"The hitter didn't know where it was, the catcher didn't know, and the umpire [Gerry Davis] didn't know. The runner crossed the plate, then everybody realized where the ball was."

Durham scored easily and the befuddled catcher, Brad Ausmus, was the loser in this zany game of hide-and-seek. In reality, according to baseball rules, once the ball was "lost," it was also, in medical terminology, DOA. And once a ball is declared dead, searching for it was pointless. As Corrales pointed out, "If it gets stuck like that, you get one base, once they figured out where the ball was." He called it one of the strangest things he'd ever seen in the majors.

RUNNING WILD

Most fans love to watch displays of power. Many fans also enjoy the speed game in baseball. Getting a chance to see a Lou Brock blaze around the bases is a thrill. One of the craziest plays involving speedy runners took place in 1985 when the Chicago Cubs were hosting the St. Louis Cardinals.

With Vince Coleman on second and Willie McGee on first, the Cards put on the double steal. Coleman stole third easily, but he ran so rapidly that he slid past the bag. Realizing he couldn't get back to third without being tagged, Coleman jumped up and dashed towards home plate.

Meanwhile, the fleet-footed McGee, who was on second, saw what had occurred and scampered for third. Amazingly, Coleman made it home, and McGee went into third unscathed. The end result, due to a unique scorer's decision, was four stolen bases on one pitch!

Don Slaught calls the next play one of the funniest moments he ever saw on a diamond. It was funny in two ways: It was "odd" funny, and it was also "gallows humor" funny.

Slaught, the catcher that day, relates what happened on July 27, 1988: "I was in New York with the Yankees when Tommy John had . . . three errors on one play. I think the ball was hit back to him; and he bobbled it for an error, then threw it wild to first for another error. The right fielder [Dave Winfield] caught the ball, threw it in. John cut if off, wheeled and threw it to me, but [he] threw it in the dugout for his third error on one play."

That play made John the first pitcher in the modern era to be guilty of three errors in an inning, and he did it all in a matter of seconds on one zany play.

A NOT-SO-GRAND SLAM

Cesar Cedeno of the Houston Astros hit what has to be one of the strangest hits, and perhaps the shortest grand slam ever. It happened on September 2, 1971, when Cedeno hit a fly ball 200 feet with the bases loaded. Two Dodgers, second baseman Jim Lefebvre and right fielder Bill Buckner, converged on the ball.

They collided, and the ball fell in safely. By the time the Dodger defense could come up with the ball, it was too late. Cedeno had already circled the bases with a rather tainted grand slam.

MORE INSIDE-THE-PARK WILDNESS

On July 25, 1998, Turner Ward came to the plate as a pinch hitter for the Pittsburgh Pirates. He faced Dennis Martinez. What followed was about as bizarre as it gets. He hit the ball down off the plate, causing it to resemble a kid on a pogo stick, bouncing up the middle.

Atlanta Braves second baseman Tony Graffanino got to the ball, but he was only able to get a glove on it. That caused the ball to change directions, caroming past center fielder Andruw Jones.

Reportedly, Jones didn't hustle after the ball when it got by him, and Ward waltzed home with a strange inside-the-park homer.

BUCK RODGERS ON THE HIT-AND-RUN WITH THE BASES FULL

Most managers wouldn't dream of calling for a hit-and-run with the bases loaded. But Buck Rodgers, who managed in the National League East when he was with the Montreal Expos, makes an exception when the situation includes certain favorable factors. Rodgers pointed out three vital elements: "A batter at the plate who usually

makes good contact, a pitcher who has good control and is usually around the plate with his pitches, and a pitcher who isn't a big strike-out pitcher."

Furthermore, the count on the batter would have to be one that would require the pitcher to come in with a strike — a count of 3-and-1, for example.

Dwight Gooden remembered a time when Don Zimmer, a much admired managerial peer of Rodgers, pulled off this trick: "One year when Zimmer was with the Cubs, with less than two outs, he sent everybody. It was the hit-and-run with the bases loaded. Lloyd McClendon was the hitter. I'd never seen that. It worked," Gooden marveled with a grin.

Such moves don't always pay off, of course. Rafael Palmeiro remembers playing for Don Zimmer when Zimmer was managing the Chicago Cubs: "I was playing . . . in '88, and we had the bases loaded in New York against the Mets. Manny Trillo was the batter, and the count was 3-and-2, I believe, when Zimmer put the hit-and-run on. Trillo swung through a pitch up in the zone, and Gary Carter caught the ball and tagged the runner for a double play, and we were out of the inning."

TWO MORE MEN'S THOUGHTS

Finally, on the topic of the bases loaded hit-and-run, the thoughts of another manager, Larry Rothschild: "I think Don Baylor did it in Colorado a couple of times [this would make sense since Zimmer served as Baylor's bench coach from 1993 to 1995]. You don't see that — the odds of it backfiring and costing you dearly are too great.

"I don't think that's having guts [to run such a play]. I think it's [a matter of] intelligence." Rothschild did concede that it depends on whether a manager such as Baylor has the right situation. "It's more of a calculated risk. If it works, great. If it doesn't, you really screwed up."

Bobby Cox disagrees. "There's nothing wrong with that strategy. Why not try something. I like that type of stuff. There's no 'book.'" He added, "It's a lot more fun." Of course, being with the successful Braves, Cox could afford to try any kind of play.

SPARKY'S HIT-AND-RUN

Another legendary manager who employed unorthodox plays at times was Sparky Anderson. Travis Fryman, who played for Anderson, said the only two men he could think of who used unique plays such as a hit-and-run with a man on third were Zimmer and Anderson.

Johnny Goryl said of Anderson, "He'd put on a hit-and-run with a runner on third so the runner could score on a ground ball. The disadvantage is if the hitter misses the ball, you're 'out to lunch,' or you could have a line-drive double play.

"The situation has to be with a contact hitter at the plate who'll put the ball in play on the ground," stated the longtime coach and manager. "Of course the count must also be favorable to the hitter — a count where the pitcher is going to throw a strike."

Frank Howard summed up the play: "What they're really doing is, rather than wait for contact to be made before you start the runner at third base, he's getting his runner in motion in case contact is made on the ground." And, if that contact is made, says Howard, "It's a walk home."

Baseball Oddities

PITCHER TURNED SLUGGER

When the 1997 season opened, Chicago Cubs center fielder Brian McRae felt safe concerning a promise he had made three years earlier. He had told teammate Frank Castillo he would buy him a Mercedes Benz if Castillo, a pitcher and notoriously poor hitter, could ever swat a home run (even during batting practice).

Well, on May 30th, Castillo, a .108 hitter, went deep twice during his rounds in the batting cage prior to a game. This hitting display pleased the man who nor-

mally couldn't hit a lick, but brought dismay and utter disbelief to McRae. When asked what he made of the whole situation, McRae simply stated, "He's still the worst hitting pitcher I've ever seen!"

DISAPPEARING BASEBALL

Larry Biittner was manning right field for the Cubs in a 1979 game against the New York Mets when another baseball performed a vanishing act. A low line drive off the bat of Bruce Boisclair came Biittner's way, but eluded his diving effort. He knew the ball had to be near him because he had deadened it when it glanced off his glove. So, he pounced off the turf and back to his feet, losing his hat during that motion.

He began looking around for the ball so the batter couldn't advance to second

base. No matter how hard he looked, no matter in which direction he gazed, he could not find the ball. It took on comic proportions as the crowd roared with delight, even as Boisclair raced past second and on towards third.

About that time Biittner, like Wagner, finally figured it out. The ball had deflected off his glove and trickled under his cap. He had found it (as a cliche goes) in the last place he looked for it. Interestingly, his timing was perfect in that he was able to throw out the runner at third.

THE BERRA BRAND OF HUMOR

Yogi Berra truly was as famous as anyone was when it came to having his own brand of baseball humor. Many of the tales of Berra are apocryphal, but remain classics, nevertheless. One little-known story deals with the time the Yankee Hall-of-Fame catcher met Robert Briscoe, the mayor of Dublin, Ireland.

Upon learning Briscoe was the city's first Jewish mayor, Berra beamed, "Isn't that great." He paused and then added in all seriousness, "It could only happen in America."

The craggy-faced Berra wasn't afraid to make himself the source of a laugh. Once a photographer told Berra to pose for a picture. "Look straight into the camera," he instructed. Berra thought for a moment, and then said, "Oh, I can't do that. That's my bad side."

PAINFUL HUMOR

An embarrassing injury took place during a 1989 exhibition game to Milwaukee Brewer Bill Spiers. He was in the on-deck circle as a close play at home plate developed. He got close to the action and began signaling to a teammate racing in from third that it was going to be a bang-bang play, and that the runner should slide into the plate. At the moment he was indicating a slide was in order, he got plunked on the head by the umpire's face mask.

The umpire wasn't out to get Spiers. He had simply flung off his mask to get a better view of the play, something umpires normally do. Observers said they had never before seen such a bizarre play.

THOU SHALL NOT WALK

In 1995, Indian catcher Tony Pena helped engineer a replication of a very famous decoy. California's Chili Davis was in the batter's box facing veteran right-hander Dennis Martinez. The count was full, at three balls and two strikes, with a runner on third.

Pena crouched behind the plate for the payoff pitch, and then suddenly stood and signaled for an intentional walk.

Seeing he was about to be given a free pass to first, Davis relaxed. And, at that moment, Martinez quickly slipped strike three by Davis. The irate batter later stated, "I got suckered. I've never seen it before and I'll never see it again."

Well, if he was watching baseball highlights a year later, he certainly did see that play executed again. On July 30, 1996, Pena, who said he performed this play once with Roger Clemens in Boston and several more times in winter ball, did it once more. This time, the victim was John Olerud, then with the Toronto Blue Jays. Martinez and Pena again worked the con game to perfection on a two-out payoff delivery.

Olerud contended he wasn't fooled as two of his coaches had yelled a warning. "Martinez made a great pitch down and away," claimed Olerud. "It might have looked like I was tricked, but I wasn't."

At any rate, the ironic part of it all is the fact that this trick is extremely famous. When Chili Davis, Tony Pena's victim in 1995, was 12 years old, the Oakland A's pulled it off during the 1972 World Series. It's almost as if Davis (and Olerud?) were proving the axiom that those who don't learn from events of the past are doomed to repeat such errors.

The World Series Deception of 1972 took place in the fifth inning of the fifth game. The A's superlative reliever Rollie Fingers was on the mound, trying to help his team cling to 4-3 lead over Cincinnati. Fingers was clearly in a jam as the Reds had Bobby Tolan leading off first base with the highly feared Johnny Bench at the plate. A few moments later, Tolan swiped second as the count reached two balls and two strikes.

It was then that the Oakland skipper, Dick Williams, went to the mound for a conference. As he strolled off the field, he pointed to first base and said, "Okay, let's put him on." Needless to say, Bench fell for it — after all, the situation obviously did call for an intentional walk. The bat lay on his shoulders as Rollie Fingers slipped a third strike past him.

Seconds later, a job well done, Fingers and his catcher Gene Tenace were jogging to the dugout as Bench stared at the plate in sheer disbelief, a strikeout casualty.

WHAT ARE THE ODDS?

Joe Niekro was a pitcher for 22 seasons in the Major Leagues. While he did possess a splendid knuckleball, allowing him to chalk up 221 victories, he was certainly not much of a hitter. Throughout his career, he could muster just one home run (on May 29, 1976). What's so odd here is his only shot came against a fellow knuckleball artist who wound up winning 318 games and who just happened to be Joe's brother, Phil.

ANNIVERSARY EVENTS

Lou Gehrig swatted his first career home run on September 27, 1923. On that same day 15 years later, he hit his final blast. That truly is an incredible coincidence.

Likewise, on September 13, 1965, Willie "The Say Hey Kid" Mays hit his 500th home run. Exactly six years later, fellow longball artist Frank Robinson launched his 500th.

Meanwhile, Eddie Mathews pelted his 500th home run on July 14, 1967. The next year on that day, longtime teammate Hank Aaron reached the 500 home run plateau. By the way, these two men hit more four baggers than any other teammate duo — even more than Babe Ruth and Lou Gehrig.

UNLIKELY EVENTS

Vic Power was a journeyman who lasted for 12 years in the majors. He was never known for his speed, stealing only 45 lifetime bases with a season high of just nine. Despite that, in August of 1958 while with Cleveland, he stole home twice in the same game. Not only that, for the entire season he wound up with just one additional stolen base.

Balks are hardly the most interesting of baseball topics. Yet there is one balk that was so unusual it's still talked about. During the All-Star game of 1961, Stu Miller, a diminutive pitcher, was on the mound for the National League. The game that year was held on San Francisco's home field, Candlestick Park.

Miller, a member of the Giants pitching staff, was well aware of the gusting winds in Candlestick. However, when one especially strong burst of wind struck him, the 165-pounder was blown off the mound. Since that movement was considered illegal, a balk had to be called on him. What was so odd about it was that it was the first balk of Miller's nine years in the majors — and he'll never live it down.

GRIDIRON OR DIAMOND?

Don Mattingly of the New York Yankees was an outstanding hitter and a fine first baseman. Even before he made it to the big leagues, scouts knew he would be a star. Still, there were several players drafted before him and, amazingly, three of them became professional football stars, forsaking the game of baseball. They were, by a strange coincidence, all quarterbacks: John Elway, Jay Schroeder and Dan Marino.

Furthermore, yet another college grid star, Rick Leach, was selected ahead of Mattingly. While the quarterbacks had a great deal of National Football League success, Leach was a bust. The only baseball organization that came out of this most unusual draft looking good was the Yankees.

THE GREAT GREG MADDUX

In 1994, Greg Maddux was almost unbeatable. His final statistics read like a line from Walter Johnson's page in the record book. The Atlanta ace went 16-6 during the strike-shortened season. Not only did he win nearly 73% of his decisions, his ERA glittered at a nearly invisible, league-leading 1.56.

In 1995, his ERA went up — to a still-microscopic 1.63. His record, however, was simply unbelievable as his ledger read 19-2 for a won-lost percentage of .905! Seldom has a pitcher dominated the game as Maddux did in that era.

Frustrated batters showed awe and respect by their actions (often shaking their heads in disbelief as they dragged themselves back to their dugouts after making outs), and their words — consider, for example, what Danny Sheaffer said.

First, though, some background. In 1995, Maddux had just gone through an especially impressive four-game stretch during which he averaged just 97 pitches per game. That worked out to an average of 10.7 pitches each inning. Further, over that stretch he walked only one batter. Two of those four games resulted in 1-0 shutouts of St. Louis. Now, the Cardinals catcher, Sheaffer, normally not much of a batter, somehow hit safely in both games. When he was asked if he had ever seen a pitcher better than Maddux, Sheaffer calmly stated that he had. "In Nintendo," he smiled. "There's a guy on my computer about that good."

A ROOKIE OF THE YEAR
WHO ALMOST WASN'T

The 1997 recipient of the Rookie of the Year Award in the National League was Philadelphia's stellar shortstop Scott Rolen. The ironic circumstance in his situation involves the fact that he came within inches of being denied the award.

It all started on September 7, 1996, when Rolen stood in the batter's box against the Chicago Cubs and pitcher Steve Trachsel. The right-hander reared back, fired the ball, and plunked Rolen with a pitch. The ball shattered Rolen's right forearm, ending his season.

At the time Rolen had chalked up 130 at bats, which just happens to be the maximum amount of trips to the plate a man can have before losing his rookie status. Had Rolen cracked a hit, or even made an out, instead of being hit with the pitch, he would have been ineligible for the rookie honors in 1997.

Only joking slightly, Rolen accepted his kudos saying, "This would be a good time to thank Steve Trachsel, who was a big part of this. At the time, I wasn't really happy with him. Now, I might give him a call and thank him."

UNANIMITY

Not only did Rolen win the Rookie of the Year Award unanimously in 1997, so did the American League winner, Boston's Nomar Garciaparra, also a shortstop. Garciaparra, whose first name is actually his father's name spelled backward (Ramon), sizzled all year long for the Red Sox.

The Rolen-Garciaparra duo marks only the third time both rookie winners were unanimous selections. The other times came in 1993 with Piazza and the American League winner, Tim Salmon of the Angels; and in 1987 when Mark McGwire won in the American League as an Oakland Athletic, and Santiago won in the National League while with the San Diego Padres.

MORE UNANIMITY

The most prestigious of all baseball's postseason awards is the Most Valuable Player. In 1997 Ken Griffey, Jr. impressed the voters so much, he won this award by gaining all 28 of the first-place votes. In doing so he became just the 13th unanimous MVP recipient. Clearly, he deserved such honors. He smacked the ball to a .304 tune while banging out 56 home runs, to lead the American League. Those 56 blasts are also among the highest single-season totals ever. In addition, he drove home 147 runs, first in the majors.

Not only that, Griffey led his league in runs with 125, total bases with 393, and slugging percentage at .646. The versatile center fielder also captured his eighth consecutive Gold Glove award.

WORLD SERIES ODDITY

When the Cleveland Indians played the Florida Marlins in the seventh game in the 1997 World Series, they gave the all-important starting assignment to Jaret Wright. What made that so unusual is: a) he hadn't even been on the 40-man roster of the Indians as of the spring of 1997; b) the son of former big-league pitcher Clyde Wright had just climbed from the low minors to the majors, all in one year; and c) his career victory total in the majors was a meager eight (no pitcher in the 93 World Series played had ever started the seventh game with fewer lifetime wins). Despite the Indians loss, Wright pitched well. He had definitely made a name for himself over the course of one highly charged season.

Incidentally, the Indians outscored the Marlins in the Series by a 44-37 margin, outhit them .291 to .272, and outpitched them with a 4.66 ERA versus a 5.48 ERA, yet lost the title to Florida. Of course, in the playoffs against the Orioles, Cleveland was outscored, yet won the pennant anyhow.

Baseball Trivia

1. Of course you remember the Marlins won the 1997 World Series in just their fifth year in existence, and the Cubbies haven't been to the Fall Classic since 1945, but can you remember how these teams fared in the Series over the last two decades?

Cleveland Indians   A. Lost two Series in the 1990s
Minnesota Twins   B. Won a Series in the 1990s
San Diego Padres   C. Won a Series in the 1980s
New York Mets   D. Lost a Series in the 1980s and the 1990s
Cincinnati Reds   E. Won a Series in the 1980s and the 1990s

Reds – B (Won 1990 Series)
Mets – C (Won 1986 Series)
Padres – D (Lost 1984 and 1998 Series)
Twins – E (Won 1987 and 1991 Series)
Indians – A (Lost 1995 and 1997 Series)

ANSWERS

---

2. If you don't know which National League team won the most regular-season games in the 1990s, you've been watching too much football. Figuring out which American League team won the most games in the decade will require more thought. Were the Yankees' strong seasons with Joe Torre at the helm enough to make up for the years in the early '90s when they struggled? How about the Indians, who also came on strong in the mid-'90s? Or could it be the steady Red Sox? What about the 1960s? The Dodgers won the World Series in 1963 and 1965, but did they win more games during the decade than the Cardinals? Looking back over the last five decades, tell us which team in each league won the most regular-season games.

DECADE	NATIONAL LEAGUE	AMERICAN LEAGUE
1950s	Dodgers (913)	Yankees (955)
1960s	Cardinals (884)	Orioles (911)
1970s	Reds (953)	Orioles (944)
1980s	Dodgers/Cardinals (825)	Yankees (854)
1990s	Braves (925)	Yankees (851)

ANSWERS

3. Somebody should sue the Yankees for unfairly monopolizing winning the World Series. In 2000, the Yanks won the Series for the 26th time, more than a quarter of all World Series. Two teams rank second with a very distant nine world championships. Some teams have only won it all once or twice since the Series was first played in 1903. Match these five teams with the number of World Series that they have won.

Chicago Cubs	A. 9
St. Louis Cardinals	B. 6
Brooklyn/Los Angeles Dodgers	C. 4
Philadelphia Phillies	D. 2
Detroit Tigers	E. 1

ANSWERS

Cubs – D
Cardinals – A
Dodgers – B

Phillies – E
Tigers – C

4. When Mitch "The Wild Thing" Williams was with the Cubs, he used to get some golfing in with his teammates, especially during spring training in Arizona. One of the Cubs was the best golfer Williams ever walked the fairway with. Another Cub is the son of an outfielder who was one of two players traded for Hank Aaron. Match these Cub teammates of Williams's with the brief bits of information we've provided.

Greg Maddux   A. Father was traded for Hank Aaron
Derrick May   B. Had three stints with the Padres; also played for the White Sox and Tigers before joining the Cubs
Paul Assenmacher   C. In top 15 on all-time games pitched list
Luis Salazar   D. Best golfer Williams ever played with
Calvin Schiraldi   E. Lost Games 6 and 7 of 1986 World Series

ANSWERS

Maddux – D
May – A (The Brewers traded Dave May and pitcher Roger Alexander to the Braves for Aaron in November 1974.)
Assenmacher – C
Salazar – B
Schiraldi – E

5. Hank Aaron never did it. Willie Mays never did it. Neither did Ted Williams nor Reggie Jackson. In fact, in the history of baseball, the feat of banging out 100 extra base hits in a season has been accomplished just eight times. One player, in the 1930s, did it twice, with 107 extra base hits in 1930 and 103 in 1932. An active player turned the trick in 1995 when he hammered 52 doubles, one triple, and 50 home runs. He came within a whisker of hitting the century mark again in 1998, as he finished with 99.

Can you pick out the old-timer who reached the 100 extra-base-hit plateau twice, and the active slugger who has almost done it twice?

A. Al Simmons and Barry Bonds
B. Chuck Klein and Moises Alou
C. Hank Greenberg and Sammy Sosa
D. Lou Gehrig and Ken Griffey Jr.
E. Hack Wilson and Juan Gonzalez

ANSWER – B

6. Here's one for you fans to debate: Who has been a better pitcher, smoke-throwing Roger "The Rocket" Clemens or Mr. Finesse, Greg Maddux?

Through 2001, which pitcher has ...

A. won more Cy Young Awards?
B. led his league in innings pitched more?
C. won more post-season games?
D. walked fewer batters per nine innings in his career?
E. won more strikeout titles?
F. a better career winning percentage?
G. won more Gold Gloves?
H. had more 20-win seasons?
I. won an MVP?
J. a better career ERA?

ANSWERS

A. Clemens (6-4)
B. Maddux (5-2)
C. Maddux (10-6)
D. Maddux (1.93-2.91)
E. Clemens (5-0)

F. Clemens (.658-.638)
G. Maddux (12-0)
H. Clemens (6-2)
I. Clemens (1-0)
J. Maddux (2.84-3.10)

7. Next time you peruse a list of Major League players and their birthplaces, take note what a large percentage of players hail from California, Puerto Rico and the Dominican Republic. You'll also see no shortage of players from Florida, Arizona, New York and Connecticut. What you won't see are many players from Alaska, Hawaii and Australia, but there are some. Match these players with their unusual birthplaces.

Curt Schilling	A. Honolulu, Hawaii
Dave Nilsson	B. Brisbane, Queensland, Australia
Chili Davis	C. Würzburg, West Germany
Ron Darling	D. Anchorage, Alaska
Mike Blowers	E. Kingston, Jamaica

ANSWERS

Schilling – D
Nilsson – B
Davis – E
Darling – A
Blowers – C

8. The following is not a typographical error: I put together a 58-game hitting streak. Don't worry, Joe DiMaggio fans, because I compiled my streak in college for Oklahoma State, and while it established an NCAA record, The Yankee Clipper's record 56-game streak remains intact. *The Sporting News* named me College Player of the Year in both

1987 and 1988, and when I left Oklahoma State, I played for the United States Olympic team in Seoul. So by the time I stepped on the Major League diamond, I had accomplished a lot. I've been no slacker in the Bigs, either. Through 2000, I've had eight 20-home run seasons and seven 90-RBI seasons. I made it into the record books in 1995 when I became the eighth player in history to hit two grand slams in one game. I can throw some leather at you also — I've won a bundle of Gold Gloves for my defense at third base.

Who am I?

ANSWER

Robin Ventura

9. You heard about a thousand times during recent home run chases that Roger Maris hit 61 homers in 1961. But how did he fare in his career other than that season?

Did he hit 50 homers in a season before or after his record-breaking year? How about 40? Did he hit 400 home runs in his career? 300? What was Roger's second-highest season home run output and lifetime home run total?

A. 39 and 275   B. 41 and 341   C. 43 and 310   D. 48 and 402   E. 53 and 368

ANSWER: A

10. There are a few things we all know about Cal Ripken Jr.: He was a fixture in the Orioles infield from 1982–2001; he broke Lou Gehrig's consecutive games record in 1995; and he'll be elected to the Hall of Fame the first year that he's eligible. Here are four more facts about the Oriole superstar, along with one statement about Cal that's not true.

Which one is it?

A. He was named MVP of two All-Star Games.
B. He won the American League Rookie of the Year Award.
C. He holds the Major League record for fewest errors in a season by a shortstop.
D. He was named MVP of the American League twice.
E. He led the Major League in home runs one season.

ANSWER

E. Ripken was named MVP of the 1991 and 2001 All-Star Games; he was the American League's Rookie of the Year in 1982; he made just three errors in 1990; and he won the American League MVP in both the 1983 and 1991 seasons. He has never led the Major League — or the American League — in home runs; 34 is his top mark (1991).

Baseball's Strangest Moments

BASEBALL: A STRANGE CAREER

In many ways baseball is one of the strangest of all careers, because a player has so short a period of time in which to earn his own place in the game.

Many potential professional ballplayers start learning the basic skills — running, throwing, hitting, fielding — when they're still of Little League age, in the primary grades at school. An early start and a fierce dedication to the game are absolutely essential. Let's say, roughly speaking, that a young man begins his pro career at the age of 18. Almost certainly he will be forced to retire 20 years later, at 38 or so. By that time he's lost his fleetness of foot, speed of reflexes, and, per-

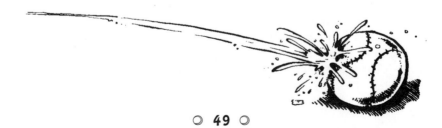

haps, sharpness of eyes, among other things. At this age men in most other professions are just beginning to hit their stride.

Actually, a 20-year pro career is exceptional — the average length of a Major League career is only 5 years. Players who can perform effectively into their late thirties and early forties (a group including Pete Rose, Darrell Evans, Tony Perez, Carl Yastrzemski, Phil and Joe Niekro, Tommy John, Hoyt Wilhelm and Nolan Ryan) are the exception rather than the rule.

Frankie Frisch, the old Hall-of-Fame second baseman, may have said it best: "When you get to the point where you really know what you're supposed to do on the ball field, you're just too damned old to be able to execute."

A legion of players have experienced serious withdrawal symptoms and faced severe psychological problems when they were forced to retire because of age. Included in this group are such stars as Ty Cobb, Babe Ruth, Joe DiMaggio, Jimmie Foxx and Willie Mays.

"When you're forced to quit after playing for 20 and more years, it's like going cold turkey," Jimmie Foxx once said. It's like withdrawing from any longtime obsession.

In closing his 22-year big league career with the New York Mets in 1973, Willie Mays grumbled to a reporter: "It's really tough to be 42, hitting .210 and sitting on the bench half the time."

This book, filled with true stories of strange moments and events, strange plays and players, batters and pitchers and strange managers and owners, shows how they all fit into this strange game, one that forces players to try to compress their careers to "make it young," for only a few can even make it, much less make it a long career.

ON MOTHER'S DAY, FELLER'S MOTHER STRUCK BY A FOUL BALL

It was a warm Mother's Day, May 14, 1939, almost cloudless throughout much of the Midwest, and an ideal day for baseball. Bob Feller, the 20-year-old fireballing phenom for the Cleveland Indians, was scheduled to face the Chicago White Sox at Comiskey Park, and for the occasion Feller's family, including his father, mother and 8-year-old sister, Marguerite, decided to drive from the homestead in Van Meter, Iowa, to Chicago, a distance of some 250 miles, to see the game.

The Fellers found themselves comfortably ensconced in grandstand seats between home and first base just before game time, and they watched as the Indians scored 2 runs in the first inning and 4 more in the third to take a 6-0 lead. Rapid Robert Feller was in rare form as he blanked the White Sox for the first two innings, not allowing a hit.

In the bottom of the third, Chicago third baseman Marvin

"Mama, watch out!"

Owen, a pinch hitter, had trouble getting around on Feller's 99-mile-an-hour fastball as he sent three straight soft fouls into the stands between first and home. On the next pitch, Owen swung late again, but this time he got the barrel of the bat on the ball and sent a vicious foul liner to the first base stands again — and to the exact spot where the Feller party was seated. There was no time to duck, and, tragically, the ball struck Mrs. Feller in the face.

As Feller followed through with his pitching motion, he could see clearly that his mother was struck by the ball. In recalling the incident years later, Feller said, "I felt sick, but I saw that Mother was conscious . . . I saw the police and ushers leading her out and I had to put down the impulse to run to the stands. Instead, I kept on pitching. I felt giddy and I became wild and couldn't seem to find the plate. I know the Sox scored three runs, but I'm not sure how.

"They immediately told me the injury was painful but not serious. There wasn't anything I could do, so I went on and finished the game and won. Then I hurried to the hospital.

"Mother looked up from the hospital bed, her face bruised and both eyes blacked, and she was still able to smile reassuringly.

"'My head aches, Robert,' she said, 'but I'm all right. Now don't go blaming yourself . . . it wasn't your fault.'" Mrs. Feller spent a couple of days in the hospital and was released feeling no ill effects.

The Indians won that Mother's Day game 9-4 as Feller ran his record to 6-1. For the entire season he went 24-9 and struck out a Major League-leading 246 batters.

In his autobiography *Strikeout Story* (New York: A. S. Barnes &

Co., 1947), Feller emphasized that his mother was always a good soldier who helped to advance his baseball career in a thousand different ways.

Feller also said later: "It was a one-in-a-million shot that my own mother while sitting within a crowd of people at a ballpark, would be struck by a foul ball resulting from a pitch I made." And on Mother's Day!

STRANGE PINCH HITTER DRAWS ROARS WITH OUTRAGEOUS STUNT

It was Sunday, August 19, 1951, at Sportsman's Park, St. Louis, as the last place Browns tangled with the Detroit Tigers, who were also deep in the second division. The game was meaningless as far as standings were concerned.

During the season Bill Veeck, flamboyant owner of the Browns, had become a bit desperate because his rag-tag team floundered badly at the gate. (Total paid admissions for the year came to a sorry 294,000.)

As the late-summer game progressed before the usual sparse Sportsman's Park crowd, Browns' manager Zack Taylor sent in a pinch hitter named Eddie Gaedel, who had never appeared in a professional game before. Tigers right-hander Bob Cain walked Gaedel on four straight pitches, and after Eddie trotted down to first, he was replaced by pinch runner Jim Delsing.

By this time the crowd was in an uproar. Pinch hitters had walked before, but none of them were as small as Gaedel, who stood 3 feet 7 inches tall and weighed 65 pounds, the normal size for a genuine midget. As Gaedel, wearing the number $1/8$ on the back of his uniform shirt, swung his 17-inch bat menacingly at Pitcher Cain, he hollered, "Throw the ball right in here and I'll moider it!"

He had been told what to do. Bill Veeck wrote in his autobiography, "I spent many hours teaching him to stand straight up, hold his little bat high and keep his feet sprawled in a fair approximation of Joe DiMaggio's classic style. I told him I'll kill him if he swings the bat."

Plate umpire Ed Hurley had questioned Gaedel's credentials as a player, but under Veeck's able direction, the midget had produced a standard Major League contract from his hip pocket.

Bill Veeck, the "Barnum of Baseball," in all his years in the game had never gone this far, and he succeeded in pulling off the greatest single outrageous stunt in the history of the game.

On the next day American League President Will Harridge turned thumbs down on any future Tom Thumbs by outlawing any further such travesty of the game.

Bill Veeck may have gained an enormous amount of notoriety for sending a midget to the plate, but nothing he did could save his franchise. After the 1953 season he was forced to sell the Browns, who in 1954 were transformed into the Baltimore Orioles.

As for Eddie Gaedel, his place in the standard baseball record books is secure. He compiled a perfect record as a pinch hitter, getting on base in his only time at bat.

FOUR HUNDRED AND NINETY-NINE PITCHES IN ONE GAME!

In a so-called "normal," nine-inning Major League baseball game, an average of 250 pitches are thrown, or some 125 by each team. If the game is a high-scoring one, or goes a few extra innings, the count may reach the 300 mark, or in rare cases, 350.

In rarer cases, however, the pitch count may reach stratospheric heights. A case in point came in the September 14, 1998, game played between the Detroit Tigers and Chicago White Sox at Tiger Stadium. This clash turned out to be a 12-inning marathon as Chicago edged Detroit 17-16 in a wild and woolly affair.

The game was knotted at 12-12 at the end of the regulation 9 innings, and then both clubs scored three runs in the 10th to push the game to 15-15. The White Sox blasted back-to-back homers from Ray Durham and Craig Wilson in the top of the 12th, while the Tigers were able to score only once in their half of the inning, and thus they were nosed out 17-16 in what appears to be a football score.

The Tigers used ten pitchers and the White Sox used eight. Their total of eighteen tied the record for most pitchers in an extra-inning game. The White Sox corps of eight hurlers threw 229 pitches, while the Tigers corps of ten moundsmen threw 270 pitches, or 499 total — a fantastic amount! That comes to at least two games' worth of pitches. The game lasted for 5 hours and 12 minutes, about twice the length of an average game.

Tabulations of pitch counts were not made until recent years, but the Elias Sports Bureau of New York (official statisticians for Major League Baseball) believe that 499 pitches is the record for any game played through 12 innings. Records for pitch counts for games played to 20 innings or so are almost impossible to arrive at.

The number of hits and runs for the Chicago/Detroit donny-brook made the pitch counts run to those high levels. Chicago batters batted out 19 base hits, while the Detroit attack came through with 22 hits. Detroit pitchers walked 11 batters, while Chicago pitchers walked only a single batsman.

The Sox starting pitcher, John Snyder, threw the first 5 innings, gave up 5 runs (4 earned), and worked his pitch count up to 92 before he was relieved. The Tigers starter, Mark Thompson, got through 4 innings, giving up 6 runs (only 2 earned) before he was sent to the showers. Interestingly, he also threw 92 pitches.

Winning pitcher for Chicago was left-hander Scott Eyre, who threw the final two innings, while the losing pitcher for Detroit was Doug Bochtler, who gave up the winning run.

Chicago's Albert Belle and Craig Wilson were the hitting stars of the game as they drove in five runs apiece. Belle banged out three doubles to go with his two singles, and went 5 for 8. Wilson, a rookie, went 4 for 7 as he homered twice and singled twice. In that high-scoring game, Belle, a 10-year veteran, passed the 1000-RBI mark.

Jerry Holtzman, veteran Chicago sportswriter, commented, "You never know what's going to happen in a Major League baseball game. Depending upon the pitching, the score might wind up at 1-0, or a football-type score at 17-16. There's no use in making pregame predictions."

AUTOGRAPH HUNTERS ARE DANGEROUS TO A PLAYER'S HEALTH!

Running the gauntlet of autograph seekers can sometimes take its toll on a ballplayer. While many diamond stars try their best to accommodate fans, there are times when the clock says if you stop and sign, you'll pay a fine. In early August, 1987, New York Yankees outfielder Claudell Washington was running late for a night game in Kansas City. He tried valiantly to dodge the autograph seekers on his way into Royals Stadium and it cost him anyway. With a small army of

"Let me get away from those fans."

clutching fans serving as an obstacle course, the trotting Washington tripped over someone's leg!

He was holding a briefcase in his left hand, and he tried using that hand to break the fall. The unhappy result was that Claudell scraped two fingers on his left hand so badly that he was unable to grip the bat properly and required more than a week on the bench before he could resume play.

The moral of this tale might be: if you're going to beat the autograph hounds, come to the park early or work on your end-around move.

OWNER STEINBRENNER, BASEBALL'S DR. JEKYLL AND MR. HYDE

In 1886, Robert Louis Stevenson published one of his best-known stories, *The Strange Case of Dr. Jekyll and Mr. Hyde.* In this horror-fantasy, Stevenson spins a tale of a man with a dual personality: Dr. Jekyll, the brilliant physician, is able to periodically transform himself into the viciously criminal Mr. Hyde. Of all the major figures in baseball today, George M. Steinbrenner III stands as, perhaps, the most controversial because of his obvious dual personality.

On the one hand, Steinbrenner is able to perform extremely magnanimous deeds, and on the other he does many perfectly awful things, though in no way do we suggest that he gets nearly as nasty as Mr. Hyde.

Before Steinbrenner became principal owner of the New York Yankees in 1973, he owned the Cleveland Pipers professional basketball team, which nearly went bankrupt, and from that point he was anxious to gain control of a major sports franchise so that he could turn it into a success. His fortune is based on his ownership of the American Shipbuilding Co., now based in Tampa, Florida. Here we'll offer a brief representative list of five "Mr. Hydes" for Steinbrenner, and five "Dr. Jekylls."

Mr. Hyde:

1. Shortly after he gained control of the Yankees, Steinbrenner showed a definite lack of knowledge of many facets of baseball. In spring training in Florida, for example, he ordered one of his players to wear his cap properly. The player did have his cap on backwards, but he was a catcher!

2. Shows an extreme lack of tolerance for a player making an error. When Bobby Murcer once muffed an outfield ground ball in a spring exhibition game, Steinbrenner blurted: "I'm paying him more than $100,000 a year and he can't catch the ball."

3. Seems to take sadistic pleasure in squashing little people. Once he had the switchboard operator in a Boston hotel fired because she wouldn't allow him to place a long distance call from the telephone in a bar, as per regulations.

4. Constantly ridicules his top players in public. He has, for example, called Dave Winfield "Mr. May" for ostensibly not performing well in late-season stretch drives — and even criticized Don

Mattingly for being "selfish" after he hit a record-tying eight homers in eight straight games in 1987. Mattingly injured his wrist shortly after this record string, and Steinbrenner blamed it on Mattingly's "exaggerated home run swing."

5. Whenever the Yankees begin playing badly, Steinbrenner pushes the panic button and starts firing, or threatening to fire, his managers and pitching coaches. Steinbrenner changed managers at least 14 times since 1973, and has had an uncounted number of pitching coaches. In 1982, when the Yankees finished a dismal fifth in the Eastern Division, Steinbrenner employed three different managers during the season: Bob Lemon, Gene Michael and Clyde King. Before Steinbrenner fires a manager, he usually embarrasses him to no end in the public press.

Dr. Jekyll:

1. Steinbrenner may fire his managers as often as some people change their socks, but he ordinarily doesn't kick them out of the Yankees organization. They remain on the payroll either as general manager, super-scout, special assistant, or coach, if they so desire — and at handsome salaries. Ex-Yankee managers who've stayed on with the organization in one capacity or another, for at least a time, include: Lou Piniella, Bob Lemon, Gene Michael, Clyde King and, of course, Billy Martin.

2. In 1979, Steinbrenner led a delegation down to Curacao in the Caribbean in order to assist the Curacao Baseball Federation, both with special instruction and a generous donation of baseball equip-

ment. Yogi Berra and Billy Martin, among others, accompanied Steinbrenner on this little publicized goodwill tour.

3. Reggie Jackson helped Steinbrenner achieve some of his greatest successes during Reggie's five years with the Yankees (1977–81) — three pennants and two World Series victories — but was let go after 1981 because he was thought to be "over the hill." However, after Jackson hit his 500th Major League homer with the California Angels in 1984, Steinbrenner presented him with a very expensive sterling silver platter commemorating the event.

4. Steinbrenner made it a point to make a special trip to Cooperstown in July 1987 to witness Jim "Catfish" Hunter's induction into baseball's Hall of Fame. Steinbrenner signed Hunter as his first major free agent in 1975, and Catfish responded by playing a major role in helping the Yankees capture three American League pennants. No one appreciates true achievement more than George.

5. George M. Steinbrenner appreciates true achievement in any field. For example, he long admired the work of George E. Seedhouse, Supervisor of Community Centers and Playgrounds in Cleveland, Ohio, during the 1950s and 1960s. And in recognition of that work he named one of his American Shipbuilding Co. iron ore carriers (a 13,000-ton vessel) the *George E. Seedhouse*.

BILL VEECK: BASEBALL'S
SHOWMAN EXTRAORDINAIRE

When Bill Veeck (as in "wreck") bought the Cleveland Indians in
1946, he took over a moribund baseball franchise that hadn't fielded
a pennant winner since 1920. With an incredible flair for showman-
ship, he succeeded in boosting the season's attendance to over
1,050,000, shattering all previous Indians' records, though the team
never managed to climb out of sixth place that year.

Veeck believed that when fans came to the ballpark they should
be entertained totally. For starters, he hired several jazz combos to
wander through the stands and perform at the end of each half-
inning.

Next, he hired former minor-league pitcher Max Patkin, a con-
tortionist, to coach occasional innings at third base. One of the
strangest-looking characters ever to wear a baseball uniform, Patkin
made it difficult for opposing pitchers to concentrate on the game as
they couldn't help watching Max twist himself in and out of pretzel
shapes along the coaching lines. Coaches rarely receive applause of
any kind, but the fans howled with glee at the sight of "Coach" Patkin,
and sometimes gave him standing ovations for his outlandish perfor-
mances.

At about the time Patkin became an Indian, Veeck signed up 33-
year-old minor-league infielder and stuntman Jackie Price as a player-
coach. Price pulled off feats never seen before on a ball field. Among

Bill Veeck (center), player-manager Lou Boudreau (right) and coach Bill McKechnie celebrate the Indians' World Series victory over the Boston Braves.

other things, he could throw two or three balls simultaneously and make them all curve, he could catch balls dropped from blimps high in the air, and even play an occasional game of shortstop for Cleveland.

One of Jackie's most memorable stunts was to suspend himself upside down from a 12-foot-high horizontal bar, grab a bat and have balls pitched to him — which he hit distances of 150 feet and more. Fans jammed their way into the park to watch Patkin and Price go through their extraordinary acts.

Bill Veeck had operated the Milwaukee Brewers of the American Association with great success in the early 1940s, and in recognition of his achievements, he was named in 1942 by *The Sporting News* as Minor League Executive of the Year. He was only 28 then. Shortly after his Milwaukee Brewers' exploits, Veeck entered the U.S. Marine Corps, was shipped off to the South Pacific, and, while stationed at Bougainville during the height of World War II, sustained a severe injury to his right leg as the result of an artillery training exercise. Unfortunately, the leg never healed properly, but during that hectic summer of '46 Veeck hobbled around through the grandstands daily, talking to the fans and getting their views as to how the Indians could be improved. Numerous times after an arduous day promoting the team, Veeck would writhe in pain at night as his leg flared up.

Infection set in and on November 1, 1946, the leg was amputated nine inches below the knee. Shortly after the operation, Veeck, still under the influence of anesthesia and quite woozy, grabbed the telephone and called Franklin Lewis, sports editor of the *Cleveland Press*, to see how the Indians came out in the Major League draft. Baseball was always on his mind.

Veeck was fitted with an artificial leg, but the pain did not disappear, and there were other operations until finally, in 1961, he had to have an amputation above the knee. During all those years he never permitted physical pain to dim his enthusiasm for baseball. On frequent occasions he removed the artificial leg and amused friends by using it as an ashtray.

"Wild Bill" as he was called by the local writers, used every sort of promotion imaginable. One night, for example, he would give the ladies orchids specially flown in from Hawaii, and on other nights he would have former Olympic track champion Jesse Owens dress up in an Indians uniform and run a foot race against one of his players. Owens, then well into his thirties, generally won.

Unpredictable "Wild Bill" suddenly sold the team (at an enormous profit) and took a year's sabbatical from baseball before he bought the St. Louis Browns in 1951. Veeck used more promotional gimmicks to draw fans into Sportsman's Park to watch his inept Browns in action: He gave away a 200-pound block of ice one night, and another time live lobsters, and in desperation he sent a midget up to the plate to pinch-hit. (See *Strange Pinch Hitter Draws Roars With Outrageous Stunt.*)

Bill surfaced again when he bought the Chicago White Sox at the end of 1958. He reached his peak as a master showman when he introduced the exploding scoreboard at Chicago's Comiskey Park. Every time a White Sox player hit a homer the scoreboard would erupt into a crescendo of sound and shoot off a fireworks rocket display. Other Major League owners were shocked and called it an "outrage," but the fans loved it. Eventually other teams in both leagues installed their own exploding scoreboards.

Veeck was forced to sell the Sox after the 1961 season because of a severe illness. He re-emerged as a big league owner for the fourth and last time in 1975, when he headed a group that again bought the financially ailing White Sox. Next, "Wild Bill" had his team wear short pants during the hot days of summer in 1976. One sportswriter fumed, "The White Sox look like an amateur softball team." However, Veeck at no time allowed his critics to hamper his highly individualistic style of running baseball teams. He spent some of his last years rooting in the bleachers, sitting bare-chested and chatting with the other fans.

Bill Veeck was elected to the Hall of Fame by the Committee of Baseball Veterans in 1991. No one during the past half-century has made a greater impact on the baseball scene.

FASTEST PITCHER?
RYAN 100.9 MPH, DALKOWSKI 108

According to the "Guinness Book of World Records," the fastest recorded Major League pitcher is Nolan Ryan, who, on August 20, 1974, while with the California Angels, threw a pitch in Anaheim Stadium, California, measured at 100.9 miles per hour.

Steve Dalkowski, little-known left-hander (b. June 3, 1939), though not generally regarded as the fastest pitcher in baseball history, threw a pitch measured at 108 miles per hour while with Elmira in the Class A Eastern League in 1962.

Dalkowski spent nine years in the minor leagues (1957–65), mostly as a Baltimore Orioles farmhand, reaching as high as Rochester and Columbus of the International League, but his wildness prevented his promotion to the majors. He was invited to spring training several times by the Orioles, but never reached his true potential despite an enormous amount of raw talent.

In those nine years in the minors, Dalkowski put together one of the strangest pitching records in professional baseball history. Over the course of 236 games, he posted a 46-80 won-lost record (.366 percentage) and pitched 995 innings, allowing only 682 base hits. He walked the gargantuan total of 1,354 batters and struck out an equally gargantuan 1,396. His ERA was a rather bloated 5.59.

Thus, in a typical game Dalkowski gave up 6 hits, walked 12 and struck out 12 to 13. If he went the distance, his game almost always took more than three hours to complete, and no one who ever paid his way into a game pitched by Steve Dalkowski ever complained about not getting his money's worth. Every game he pitched was a dramatic event.

While with Stockton of the Class A California League in 1960, he pitched 170 innings in 32 games, won 7 games, lost 15, allowed only 105 hits, walked 262 and struck out 262! Obviously he was very hard to hit.

Dalkowski's great left arm began giving out before he was 27, and from that point on, his journey through life was not altogether happy. He worked for a time as a migratory laborer in California's vineyards and had long bouts with John Barleycorn.

In 1978, the Society for American Baseball Research (then based in Cooperstown, New York) honored Dalkowski by including him in a newly published biographical and statistical volume entitled *All-Time Minor League Baseball Stars.*

GEORGE BLAEHOLDER, FATHER OF THE SLIDER

George Blaeholder ran up a mediocre 104-125 record as a right-handed pitcher in the American League from 1925 to 1936, but he is credited with having been the first pitcher to throw the slider, one of the most difficult of all pitches to hit. He threw his first slider with the St. Louis Browns in 1928, and generously passed on his technique to other pitchers.

The slider takes off like a fastball, but then curves sharply just before it reaches the batter. Batters have scornfully referred to the slider as a "nickel curve." The pitch really didn't have a major impact upon baseball until the 1950s and 1960s.

Stan Musial, one of the greatest batters of all time (he banged out 3,630 base hits and averaged .331 in a 23-year career, 1941–63), once said, "I could have hit better in the latter years of my career and stayed around a while longer if it hadn't been for the slider."

IT DIDN'T PAY TO MESS
WITH BURLY EARLY WYNN

Early Wynn, the Hall-of-Fame right-hander who piled up a 300-244 won-lost record over 23 big league seasons (1939–63, with time out for World War II service), looked as mean as a junkyard dog when he took the mound. He had his own special way of intimidating hitters. Most batters were afraid to dig in on "Burly Early" because they never knew when his brush-back pitch was coming.

One reporter commented that Early would knock down his own grandmother if she ever crowded the plate. Fortunately, she never had the opportunity of batting against her grandson. However, when Early was nearing the end of the trail with the Chicago White Sox in the early 1960s, he pitched against his 17-year-old son, Early, Jr., in batting practice. Well, Early, Jr., socked one of his dad's best pitches up against the bleacher wall. What do you suppose happened when the boy dug in for his father's next delivery? He was sent flying on his derriere, of course, in order to avoid the high, hard one.

One time Early was asked to name the toughest batter he ever faced. Wynn replied without a moment's hesitation, "There were two guys . . . one was named Hillerich and the other was Bradsby."

That meant Early's enemy was anyone with a bat in his hands.

PETE ROSE: SLUGGER BEGAN
AT AGE 3, WASTED VALUABLE YEARS
IN HIGH SCHOOL

Pete Rose's father Harry was anxious to get his first-born son started in baseball at the earliest possible age, so little Pete began at just 2 years to catch thrown balls. When Pete was 3 he started out as a slugger. The first time he remembers slugging he connected solidly with a pitch served up by his dad, and drove a hard rubber-coated ball to right-center field, over and out of the backyard ball field and against a glass windowpane that promptly cracked in the kitchen of the Rose home on Braddock Avenue in Cincinnati.

That long drive by the Cincinnati Red, who holds baseball's all-time career record of 4,256 hits, was swatted on a summer Saturday in 1944. The crack is still in the window. According to a July 7, 1987, *New York Times* report, LaVerne Noeth, Pete's mother, was standing in the kitchen that day more than four decades ago when she heard the glass crack.

"My husband said, 'Hon, come here, look where Pete hit the ball,'" Mrs. Noeth recalled recently. "He said, 'I don't want it fixed. I'm going to show people where he hit that ball.' Pete was so small then, he was always small."

Little has changed in the neighborhood. Braddock Avenue is still a clump of homes on a hill above the Ohio River, five miles west of downtown, and boys still play ball there. At the old Rose household, members of Pete's family have no trouble finding first base in the backyard although the ball field is now covered with honeysuckle shrubs and black locust trees.

After he hit that storied backyard liner at the age of 3, Pete Rose continued playing ball at a furious pace, and he became so involved in various sandlot leagues that it took him five years to get through high school in Cincinnati. By having to spend that extra year, Pete didn't start his pro career with Geneva, N.Y., of the New York-Penn League until he was 19 in 1960, when others began at 18.

If he had started in the minors a year earlier, he might have had an additional season in the big leagues and broken even

"What a boy, what a batter, that Pete."

more records. Pete didn't fail in high school because he was a bad student, mind you. His I.Q. had been measured as high as 150.

BABE RUTH: BEATS WHOLE AMERICAN LEAGUE IN HOME RUN PRODUCTION

Home run hitting hit a peak in the Major Leagues in 1987 as 27 players hit for the circuit 30 or more times. Recent years have seen the single-season home run record shattered twice. Although there are many sluggers going for many homers, still there is no single slugger who dominates the long ball game as Babe Ruth did during the 1920s.

Ruth, in fact, on two separate occasions, in 1920 and 1927, personally hit more homers than each of the seven other teams in the American League. In 1920, the "Sultan of Swat" smacked out a record 54 homers and no team in the league matched that total. St. Louis came the closest with 50, followed by Philadelphia with 44; Chicago, 37; Washington, 36; Cleveland, 35; Detroit, 30; and Boston, 22.

In 1927, the Bambino reached the peak of his long ball power as he whacked a record 60 homers, and that year no single AL team managed to top that total. Philadelphia "threatened" Ruth with 56 four baggers, followed by St. Louis with 55; Detroit, 51; Chicago, 36; Washington, 29; Boston, 28; and Cleveland, 26.

No other Major League player has come close to matching this particular home run achievement of George Herman Ruth.

Most veteran baseball observers believe that no one could hit a baseball harder or farther than Babe Ruth when he was at his peak with the New York Yankees from 1920 to the early 1930s. Ruth's longest homer may well have been a 600-foot shot he belted in a spring exhibition game at Tampa in 1925.

No one ever measured the velocity of his drives, but pitcher Mel Harder, who came up with the Cleveland Indians in 1928, recalled the days when the Bambino batted against him at Cleveland's old League Park. This vintage-style ballpark (now torn down) had a concrete wall topped by a wire fence running from right field to right-center field. "Ruth's drives often hit that concrete right-field wall with such tremendous force that the ball would bounce all the way back to second base," Harder said. "Those balls would usually have to be thrown out of the game because they came back a bit flattened and carried a spot of green paint from the wall," he added.

JOE DIMAGGIO: ALWAYS ONE TOUGH HOMBRE TO STRIKE OUT

Most baseball experts feel that the greatest single achievement in baseball was Joe DiMaggio's hitting in 56 straight games in 1941. We beg to differ on this point — in our opinion, Joe D's most remarkable accomplishment was striking out only 369 times in his Major League career in approximately 8,000 total times at bat (including walks, sac flies, hit by pitcher, etc.).

Amazingly enough, Joltin' Joe hit 361 homers in his 13 years with the New York Yankees (1936–51, with three years out for World War II military service), a figure only 8 fewer than his total strikeouts! In his rookie year, DiMag fanned on 39 occasions, and he never again struck out that many times in a season.

From that point on, DiMaggio enjoyed six seasons in which he had more homers than K's. Here are the fantastic figures, with homers first and strikeouts second: 1937 — 46, 37; 1938 — 32, 21; 1939 — 30, 20; 1940 — 31, 30; 1941 — 30, 13; 1946 — 25, 24; and 1948 — 39, 30. The "Yankee Clipper" almost made it again in 1950 when he slammed 32 homers against 33 strikeouts.

Even Bob Feller, baseball's unrivaled strikeout king from the mid-1930s through the 1940s, had a tough time fanning DiMaggio. Joe D, who had a career batting average of better than .320 against Feller, once told us:

"Feller is best known for his great fastball, of course, but he also had a wicked curve which made him extremely effective. At the same time, he was a proud man and never tried too many curves against me . . . He almost always tried to blow the fastball by me — and since I pretty much knew what to expect I never had too much trouble with him."

We should emphasize here that DiMaggio never struck out much against anybody because he had extremely quick reflexes, perfect coordination and keen eyesight.

MIZE AND TED WILLIAMS VERY TOUGH TO STRIKE OUT

Three times in his career Johnny Mize posted records where his homers topped the totals of his whiffs. While with the New York Giants in 1947, the big left-handed-hitting first baseman bashed a career-high 51 homers and fanned only 42 times — and in the following year he hit for the circuit 40 times against only 37 strikeouts.

In 1950, as a member of the New York Yankees, Mize homered 25 times against 24 strikeouts. Overall, in a 15-year big league career (1936–53, with three years out for World War II military service), Mize rang up 359 homers against 524 strikeouts, an excellent ratio.

"I never swung crazy," Mize told us recently. "If the pitch was out of the strike zone, I just didn't go for it . . . I always tried to wait for my pitch," he disclosed.

Ted Williams, who possessed extraordinary vision, and who knew how to control a bat as well as anyone in baseball, had four seasons in which his homers outnumbered his strikeouts. In this listing the homers are given first: 1941 — 37, 27; 1950 — 28, 21; 1953 — 13, 10; and 1958 — 28, 24. Overall, in a 19-year career (1939–60, with three years out for World War II military service), Williams hit 524 homers as opposed to 709 strikeouts, a superb ratio.

BILL DICKEY: DIDN'T TAKE MANY THIRD STRIKES EITHER

Bill Dickey, the Hall-of-Fame New York Yankees catcher, is another throwback to an earlier era when some of the game's top power hitters were hard to fan. Though he didn't hit as many homers as

DiMaggio, Mize or Williams, he still managed to have five seasons when his homers exceeded his strikeouts, and once when they were even (in 1933 he had 14 homers and 14 strikeouts).

Those five sterling Dickey seasons are (homers first): 1932 — 15, 13; 1935 — 14, 11; 1936 — 22, 16; 1937 — 29, 22; and 1938 — 27, 22. In 17 seasons with the Yankees (1928–46, with two years out for World War II military service), Bill Dickey rapped out 202 homers against only 289 strikeouts.

Said Dickey, years after his playing days: "In many ways baseball today is strange to me because so many big-leaguers — or supposed big-leaguers — are lunging at the ball in trying to get distance, and they're striking out 3, 4 and even 5 times a game in the process."

"SHOELESS" JOE JACKSON: MORE TRIPLES THAN STRIKEOUTS

While with the Chicago White Sox in 1920, Joe Jackson accomplished a feat that would be virtually impossible for a modern player to match — he actually had more triples than strikeouts, 20 to 14. While with the Cleveland Indians in 1912, "Shoeless" Joe lined out 26 triples, but we don't know if his three-baggers outnumbered his whiffs because strike-out records were not kept until 1913.

Compared to Joe Jackson, Dale Mitchell, who was active from 1946 to 1956, was a "modern" player in the strict sense. In any event, Mitchell was the last Major Leaguer, according to our best calculations, to triple more times than strike out in a single season. While with the Cleveland Indians in 1949, Mitchell, a left-handed slap hitter, tripled 23 times against only 11 strikeouts, a better than a 2-1 ratio. Fantastic!

Sam Crawford, the all-time triples leader with 312, had one season we know about where his three-baggers exceeded his strikeouts: 1916 — 13, 10. ("Wahoo Sam" was with the Detroit Tigers at the time). Crawford may have had other triples-over-whiffs seasons, but Crawford's strikeout totals while he was with Cincinnati and Detroit from 1899 through 1912 were not kept.

Ty Cobb may have had at least one triples-over-whiffs season, but his 1907–1912 strikeout figures also are shrouded in mystery.

FIRST (ILLEGAL) USE OF A DESIGNATED HITTER

There were mutterings for a DH rule as far back as the 1930s. Hitting was the dominant factor in baseball in the 1930s and 8 batters out of 9 got the job done, so the DH idea failed to take hold. Then much later, pitchers began to rule the game and scores were low, so the pitcher's turn at bat became more important.

Interestingly, several informal and abortive attempts at using a DH were made many years before the rule was officially adopted by the American League in 1973. For example, a little known exception was made in 1939 when Chicago White Sox pitcher Bill "Bullfrog"

Dietrich found himself struggling during the course of a hot mid-summer afternoon against the Cleveland Indians at Comiskey Park, Chicago. Sox manager Jimmy Dykes went over to Cleveland manager Oscar Vitt and asked him if it was all right with Vitt if Dykes used a pinch hitter for Dietrich but allowed Bullfrog to remain in the game. "It's okay with me if it's okay with the umpires," said the gentlemanly Vitt.

The pinch hitter was used and Dietrich remained in the game!

STILL A REGULAR AT 44 — YAZ SETS MARK FOR LONG CAREER

Carl Yastrzemski starred for the Boston Red Sox for 23 years, and in 1983, at the age of 44, he became the oldest player in modern big league history to play regularly. Though "Yaz" was an outfielder for most of his career, he saw service mostly as a designated hitter in 1983 — his final season — as he played in 119 games, collecting 101 base hits and batting a respectable .266.

In sporting the Red Sox uniform for nearly a quarter century, Yastrzemski set an American League record by playing in the most games — 3,308 — and registering the most times at bat — 11,988 — while slamming out 3,419 base hits, good for a solid .285 lifetime batting average. He also won three batting championships (including a "Triple Crown' in 1967 when he swatted .326, bashed 44 homers and drove in 121 runs). He also tied a Major League record by playing in

100 or more games for 22 seasons, and led the American League in intentional walks — 190.

He was elected into baseball's Hall of Fame at Cooperstown in 1989, his first year of eligibility.

Carl Yastrzemski's endurance records were subsequently tied and/or broken by Pete Rose of the Cincinnati Reds. In 1985, the 44-year-old Rose, by then the Reds manager, played in 119 games (mostly at first base), tying Yaz, and in 1986, at the age of 45, he played semi-regularly (72 games) at first before he benched himself permanently (as it turned out) in mid-August.

SCOTT SETS CONSECUTIVE GAME RECORD BEFORE BEING BENCHED FOR WEAK HITTING

Everett "Deacon" Scott, a native of Bluffton, Indiana, broke into the Major Leagues in 1914 with the Boston Red Sox as a 21-year-old short-stop, and just over two years later, on June 20, 1916, began one of the most remarkable streaks in baseball history. From that day through the 1921 season, he never missed a game with the Red Sox — over 800 of them.

After the 1921 campaign, Scott went to the New York Yankees in a multi-player trade, and from that point continued his "Iron Man" role. A fine fielder, he went more than three additional seasons, never missing being in the lineup through May 5, 1925. This ran his streak of consecutive games played to 1,307. Scott, a runt of a man standing 5 feet 8 inches and weighing 150 pounds, but an extremely durable athlete, became the first man in professional baseball to play more than 1,000 games in a row.

Scott could have gone on to extend his streak even further but Yankees manager Miller Huggins had to bench him for weak hitting! The Yankees in those years with Babe Ruth were called "Murderers' Row" and Scott batted around .250.

Interestingly, Scott's teammate, the hard-hitting, 22-year-old first baseman named Lou Gehrig, began his own record-breaking streak of 2,130 straight games on June 1, 1925, less than a month after the Little Deacon was benched.

In early August 1925, Scott was sent to the Washington Senators on waivers and finished his big league career with the Chicago White Sox and Cincinnati Reds in 1926. Everett Scott ended with a career batting average of a modest .249 in 1,654 Major League games, but had remained in the lineup on a daily basis so long because of his sure-handed fielding. He led American League shortstops in fielding percentage for a record eight years, all in succession, 1916 through 1923.

BATTING AVERAGES HIT BOTTOM—
ONLY ONE .300 HITTER IN AL

By the middle 1960s hitting in the majors, especially in the American League, had declined so much that the lords of baseball decided something had to be done. The low point for hitting came in 1968 when the ten American League teams posted a combined batting average of .230. The Minnesota Twins took the team batting crown with a "robust" .240, while the New York Yankees finished last with an anemic .214 mark. Carl Yastrzemski of the Boston Red Sox had the distinction of being the AL's only .300 hitter, taking the batting crown with a .301 average, the lowest average for a batting leader in Major League history.

The National League did a bit better as their ten teams combined for a .243 batting mark.

By contrast, in 1930, considered to be a peak year for Major League hitting, the eight American League teams posted a combined .288 mark, while the eight National League clubs swatted .303. The New York Giants led the parade with a very substantial .319 team average.

STRANGE DEMISE OF THE METS . . .
A LITTLE BIRD DID THEM IN

The New York Mets in 1986 dominated baseball as they posted a glittering 108-54 won-lost mark in, finishing first in the National League's Eastern Division 21½ games ahead of the second-place Philadelphia Phillies. The Mets went on to defeat the Houston Astros, the NL's Western Division Champs, four games to two in the League Championship Series, and climaxed their amazing season by whipping the Boston Red Sox four games to three in a dramatic World Series. The Mets reigned supreme as baseball's world champions.

The 1987 New York Mets never seemed to get off on the right foot as they went on to disappoint their fans by finishing second in the NL East, five games behind the St. Louis Cardinals. All sorts of strange happenings prevented the Mets from reaching the top for a second straight season.

For starters, Ray Knight, their star third baseman and World Series MVP, defected to the Baltimore Orioles after a contract dispute, and Dwight Gooden, their top pitcher, spent the first two months in a drug rehab clinic. Several other key pitchers, including Bob Ojeda and Rick Aguilera, were out for long spells with injuries.

However, the strangest incident of all, and one that typified the Mets' ill luck in 1987, occurred at the Sunday, April 12 game at Shea Stadium, when the '86 champs faced the Atlanta Braves. Dion James, Braves outfielder, hit a fly ball toward left-center field, but before any

Met could catch up to it, the ball struck and killed a pigeon in full flight. Both the ball and pigeon dropped down onto the field in a thud and James was awarded a ground-rule double. The Mets went on to lose that game 11-4.

When Rafael Santana, Mets shortstop, picked up the dead bird in his hand, he muttered, "We're not getting any breaks at all."

BLUE JAYS SET NEW RECORD, HAMMER 10 HOMERS IN ONE GAME

"I don't think anyone threw well. It was an embarrassing baseball game . . . I'm not the only one embarrassed. Everybody in the clubhouse is embarrassed," moaned Baltimore Orioles' manager Cal Ripken, Sr., after his team was devastated 18-3 by the Toronto Blue Jays at Toronto's Exhibition Stadium on Monday, September 14, 1987.

What made the game particularly embarrassing for the Orioles was Toronto's awesome display of home run power. The Blue Jays hammered out 10 "dingers," breaking the Major League record of 8 in one game. (The New York Yankees of 1939 set that mark the first time when they blasted 8 roundtrippers against the Philadelphia A's. A number of other teams have since hit that figure.)

Blue Jays' catcher Ernie Whitt began the home run parade when he led off the second inning with a shot into the right-field bleachers. Whitt, a 6-foot-1-inch, 200-pound left-handed pull hitter, belted another solo homer in the fifth inning, and added a 3-run poke in the seventh. (A number of renowned home run hitters, including Hank Greenberg, never hit 3 in a single game.)

Left fielder George Bell and third baseman Rance Mulliniks each contributed two homers to the onslaught. Center fielder Lloyd Moseby hit one out of the park and his late-inning replacement, rookie Rob Ducey, also got into the act with a drive into the right-field seats. Designated hitter Fred McGriff, also a rookie, made it an even 10.

Baltimore Mike Hart, a rookie center fielder, saved face for the Orioles slightly when he hit for the circuit in the third inning, making it 11 homers for the two teams, tying the all-time single game record set by the Yankees with six, and the Detroit Tigers, five, in 1950.

SUPER FAN MISSED ONLY ONE WORLD SERIES GAME IN 42 YEARS

C. E. "Pat" Olsen, a 6-foot-2-inch right-handed power pitcher, signed a contract with the New York Yankees in 1923 as a 20-year-old and was fully expected by the Yankees to become a star.

For the next five years Olsen labored in the minor-league vineyards with stops at Des Moines, Pittsfield and Springfield, Massachusetts, St. Joseph, Missouri, Atlanta, and Amarillo, Texas.

"In 1924, I roomed with Lou Gehrig at the Yankees spring training complex at St. Petersburg, Florida, and thought I was ready at that time to make the big leagues, but I was sent back down to the minors just before the season began," Olsen reminisced. "After my last stop with Amarillo of the Western League in 1927, I decided to call it quits as a ballplayer because by that time I knew I wouldn't make it to the majors. . . . Then I got into the oil business in Texas," Olsen added.

Over the years Olsen became an oil millionaire, but his passion for baseball continued unabated. In 1933 he attended the Major League's first All-Star Game played at Chicago's Comiskey Park, and from then through 1987 he never missed seeing any of the 58 mid-summer classics. Olson died in May, 2000, but he reported in 1987 that he'd attended nearly 300 World Series games — in fact, from 1938 until 1980, Pat witnessed 255 consecutive World Series contests, missing the final game of the Kansas City–Philadelphia Series (in Philadelphia) because of a vital business commitment. That's the only Series game he failed to see in nearly 50 years. In 1987, he had been to every Hall of Fame Induction Ceremony at Cooperstown since 1939.

"I doubt very much if any other fan has compiled an attendance record of this magnitude," observed Bob Fishel, Executive Vice President of the American League and a baseball executive with more than 40 years experience.

"I never made more than $300 a month as a minor league player, but once I established myself in business and had the time and resources to travel, I made up my mind not to miss a single one of baseball's premier events," said Pat Olsen. The Aggies of Texas A&M University in College Station, Texas, honored him by naming their baseball park Olsen Field.

BABE'S SIGNATURE WORTH $500, BUT BEWARE! SOME PHONY

It is estimated that Babe Ruth signed at least two million autographs during his lifetime. With only a small fraction of those autographs being extant, values of genuine Ruth signatures are climbing steadily. A Ruth signature on a baseball generally sells for $500 and more.

Collectors should beware, though, because Ruth autographs have been widely counterfeited.

Mel Ott, the Hall-of-Fame New York Giants home run hitter, didn't mind autographing for fans since his name consists of only six letters. "Master Melvin" got to a point where he could sign 500 autographs per hour.

LUKE APPLING FIELDS A COFFEE POT AT CHICAGO'S COMISKEY PARK!

Luke Appling, the Hall-of-Fame shortstop, had a big league playing career spanning 20 seasons (1930–1950, with a year out, 1944, for military service) and was known as a great raconteur. He was a baseball "lifer": he managed and coached a long series of major and minor-league teams until his passing at the age of 84 in 1991.

Appling made sports headlines in the summer of 1985, when, at the age of 78, he slammed a home run into the left field stands at Washington D.C.'s Robert F. Kennedy Stadium during an old-timer's

game. Who threw the gopher ball? Why, it was none other than Hall-of-Famer Warren Spahn, who was a sprightly 64 at the time. After the game, Spahn said, "Appling hit the homer on a hanging curve."

About a year after Appling blasted that "senior home run," we had a chance to interview him at length at a major card show staged in Los Angeles. We asked Luke what was the strangest experience he ever had on a big league baseball diamond.

With only a moment's hesitation Appling replied, "The old Comiskey Park in Chicago was built over a rubbish dump. That means the entire baseball diamond consisted of landfill. In my first full season as a White Sox regular in 1931, we were playing the Detroit Tigers and I think it was the Tigers second baseman, Charley Gehringer, who hit a hot ground ball down to short and I dug deep into the ground in trying to pick up the ball. I didn't come up with the ball, but I did bring up a rusty old coffee pot that had been buried years before the park was completed!

"The next day the team's ground crew laid down a thick layer of fresh topsoil over the infield so that players at Comiskey could concentrate on picking up baseballs rather than rusty old trash."

LARRY LAJOIE'S 1901 BATTING AVERAGE ZOOMS FROM .401 TO .422

Larry Lajoie, the great-fielding, hard-hitting second baseman who played in the majors for 21 years (from 1896 through 1916), won the American League batting crown in 1901 with a purported .401 average while with the Philadelphia Athletics.

Of course, a .401 average for a full season is super, but in reality Lajoie did even better. Some 50-odd years later statisticians, led by the eagle-eyed Cliff Kachline, discovered that through mistakes in addition, Lajoie was short-changed by nine hits. He actually piled up 229 base hits, including 48 doubles, 13 triples, and a league-leading 14 homers, and that boosted his average by 21 points, from .401 to .422. That .422 still stands as the highest seasonal average by an American Leaguer. (Ty Cobb's .420 in 1911 and George Sisler's .420 in 1922 now rank second.)

After the conclusion of the 1901 season, league statisticians just didn't add up Lajoie's hit total correctly — his at-bats remained the same at 543, and the nine additional base hits raised his lifetime big league average by one point, from .338 to .339.

EDD ROUSH'S 48-OUNCE BAT

Edd Roush, whose career spanned the 1913–1931 period and who was one of the greatest all-around players in the National League, was such a ferocious competitor that he became known as "The Ty Cobb of the National League." Roush entered the Hall of Fame in 1962, with many baseball historians maintaining that he should have been given his bronze plaque at Cooperstown much earlier.

Roush's brilliant career was marked by one peculiarity: he used a 48-ounce bat, the heaviest bat ever used by a Major League player. Contemporary players generally use bats weighing from 32 to 34 ounces, while a number even use 31-ouncers, even sluggers. The ballplayer of today feels he can gain greater bat speed with a lighter piece of lumber, enabling him to drive the baseball a greater distance.

As Roush approached his 80th birthday, he said, "I hit very different from the way they hit today. I don't believe anyone used a bat heavier than the 48-ounce type I had. It was a shorter bat, with a big handle, and I tried to hit to all fields. Didn't swing my head off, just used a snap swing to make contact and drive the ball."

Roush retained his batting style and his 48-ounce wooden bat even though the lively ball came into being in 1919–1920 and other players went for much lighter clubs to generate more bat speed in order to hit for distance.

His tactics obviously paid off, because Edd Roush won two National League batting championships while with the Cincinnati Reds in 1917 and 1919, averaging .341 and .321, respectively. In 1967 big league games he averaged .323 and piled up 2376 base hits. While he managed only 67 home runs, he hit 339 doubles and 183 triples, the latter being a very lofty stat.

DAVE KINGMAN—
FOUR TEAMS IN ONE SEASON!

David Arthur Kingman, a 6-foot-6-inch, 220-pound home run slugger, slammed out 442 circuit blasts during his checkered 16-year big league career (1971–1986), and that gives him the distinction of having the most homers for a player not in baseball's Hall of Fame.

Throughout his tenure in the big leagues, Kingman was noted for not speaking with reporters and being generally hostile to the press as a whole. Early on, after he reached the majors with the San Francisco Giants in 1971, he claimed he was badly misquoted after giving out a series of interviews. And because of his generally ornery personality, Kingman went from one team to another, playing for a total of seven teams in both Major Leagues.

He was signed out of the University of Southern California by the San Francisco Giants and he debuted with the parent club late in the 1971 season. Just before the start of the 1975 campaign, Kingman was sold to the New York Mets. By that time he had worn out his welcome with the Giants.

Big Dave remained with the Mets for the entire 1976 season, and then in '77 he really hit the jackpot for changing teams. In that year he played for exactly four of them. He went to the San Diego Padres in a June 15 trade, then on September 6 he was sold on waivers to the California Angels. His tenure with the Angels lasted for exactly 9 days because on September 15 he was sold to the New York Yankees. Yes, he did remain with the Yanks for the remainder of the season: 2 whole weeks. Baseball historians found that seeing service with four big league teams within a single season at least ties a record.

The Yankees had no interest in signing Dave for 1978, and so the big slugger signed with the Chicago Cubs, where he remained, remarkably enough, for three full seasons.

Though he was on the disabled list for nearly a month in '78, Dave still managed to hit 28 homers in 119 games. In '79, when many baseball experts said that Dave was nearing the end of the road, he surprised everybody by having a "career year" as he led the league with 48 homers and 115 runs batted in while averaging a solid .288 — all career highs for him. Dave's fortune declined in 1980 as he went on the disabled list three times, but when he was on the diamond he did play well, batting .278 in 81 games with 18 homers.

The Cubs soured on Kingman for a variety of reasons, particularly because of one grisly incident. He took a strong dislike to one female Chicago baseball reporter and expressed his displeasure with her writing by placing an expired rodent in her handbag.

Dave went over to the New York Mets at the beginning of 1981, and though he was happy about getting back to his old club, he again spent a bit of time on the DL, and was also benched at various times for striking out too much. Though he averaged .221 in 100 games, he did manage to slam 22 homers. The Mets knew that Kingman was a big gate attraction, a real threat at the plate. Moreover, fans liked to see his 450- to 500-foot "homers" into the stands during batting practice.

"King Kong" Kingman tried mightily to mend his ways in '82, and he kept himself off the bench by showing sporadic and game-winning bursts of power. While he averaged a skinny .204 (going 109 for 535 in 149 games), he led the league with 37 circuit blasts and drove in 99 runs. No other player has led the league in homers with that low an average. A free and sometimes wild swinger, Dave struck out a league-leading 156 times. Dick Young, then a baseball writer for the *New York Daily News,* and long one of Dave's severest critics, called him "King Kong Kingman, The Strikeout King."

Kingman went on to have a career-worst season in '83 as he "rode the pines" for long periods. He batted less than his weight, 198 in 100 games, and homered only 13 times.

He certainly wasn't ready to quit baseball at that point. After his release by the New York Mets, he signed with the Oakland Athletics in

1984, and remained with the A's for three full seasons, retaining his reputation as an authentic home run threat. In those 3 years he hit exactly 100 homers — 35, 30 and 35, respectively. His 1984 stats were particularly good: he averaged a strong .268 and knocked in 118 runs. Kingman was miffed that he didn't make the American League All-Star team in 1984, although he did play in the 1976 and 1980 All-Star games.

After being released by the A's following the '86 season, Kingman still had visions of reaching the magic 500 home run mark, and tried making a comeback in July '87 by signing with Phoenix of the Triple A Pacific Coast League. But after 20 games, with a sub-standard .203 average and only 2 homers, Dave hung up his uniform for good.

There are still those baseball writers who are long ball aficiona-dos and feel Kingman is Hall-of-Fame material, despite his .236 life-time batting average in the majors. They also point to his 1210 runs batted in and his home run ratio of 6.6% (measured against official times at bat) — a stat good enough to give him a fifth-place spot on the all-time list among retired players. Dave's detractors point to his 1816 strikeouts — another fifth-place all-time rating.

We had the opportunity to interview Dave Kingman in October 1998. Frankly, we've never encountered a more affable and approach-able interviewee. Said Kingman, "I may not have liked sportswriters when I was playing, and though I may have been a bit tough to get along with, I've always felt I was a decent person. Maybe I got a less-than-excellent reputation early in my career, but I was young, maybe a bit immature, but I have grown up. Remember, there are real pressures in playing big league baseball. Some basically excellent players fold because they cannot handle the pressure and play at their best before big and noisy crowds. I've felt that most baseball fans are fair and decent to the players, but the noisy boo-birds can get under your skin and warp your personality. By the same token, baseball writers in general are decent guys, but there are those who rip you all the time, and that kind of stuff can affect you. In general, I had a good career and have no regrets. Playing big league baseball is a rough and tumble profession."

AVERAGE LIFE OF A MAJOR LEAGUE BASEBALL IS ONLY SIX PITCHES!

During Major League baseball's so-called "Stone Age," the late 1870s up to the turn of the century, a ball stayed in the game until it became so discolored, or even misshapen, that it had to be thrown out for a replacement. There are even confirmed reports that a single baseball was used for an entire game back in those days! In fact, the use of beat-up balls continued to be a practice in the big leagues up to around the World War I period.

Edd Roush, a National League outfielder, heavy hitter, and Hall of Famer, often spoke of mashed-up baseballs being used in championship games. He spoke of this in great detail in an interview that appeared in Lawrence S. Ritter's landmark book *The Glory of Their Times,* published in 1966.

Roush, who played in the majors from 1913 to 1931, mostly with the Cincinnati Reds and New York Giants, recalled, "Until 1919, they had a dead ball. Well, the only way you could get a home run was if the outfielder tripped and fell down. The ball wasn't wrapped tight and lots of times it'd get mashed on one side.

"I've caught many a ball in the outfield that was mashed flat on one side. Come bouncing out there like a jumping bean. They wouldn't throw it out of the game, though. Only used about three or four balls in a whole game. Now they use 60 or 70. "

Roush had that just about right. A recent study by Major League Baseball indicates that the average ball has a life of only about six pitches in a game. Rawlings Sporting Goods, Inc., based in Saint Louis, supplies all the baseballs used by the thirty teams making up the American and National Leagues. Those thirty teams gobble up 720,000 baseballs every season, according to Rawlings. A baseball retails for $6, but the Major Leagues buy them up at wholesale prices.

Mark McGwire, the St. Louis Cardinals slugger, hit a lot of homers out of the park, but even when he connected 60 or 70 times in a season, that amounted to only a fraction of the baseballs lost in action. And that says nothing of the many baseballs McGwire hits out of the park in batting practice. McGwire, in fact, draws crowds of fans who want to see him blast baseballs into the bleachers and over the stands in batting practice.

Rawlings Sporting Goods also supplies baseballs to most of the minor league teams, as well as to thousands of amateur teams scattered across the United States. Virtually all of the Rawlings baseballs are made overseas, particularly in Haiti, where the company takes advantage of low-priced labor. Baseball manufacture is labor intensive because the balls must be hand-stitched. Neither Rawlings nor any other company has been able to develop machinery to stitch baseballs on an assembly-line basis. The work must be done with human hands.

WHEN IS A RECORD NOT REALLY A RECORD?

When George Edward "Rube" Waddell, the brilliant but eccentric Philadelphia Athletics left-hander, struck out a supposed total of 343 batters in 1904 (Rube went 25-19 in 384 innings of work), that posting stood as a Major League record for decades.

Fast-forward to the 1946 season when Bob Feller, fireballing right-hander of the Cleveland Indians, went on a strikeout binge and wound up with 348 Ks in 371 innings of work as he went 26-15.

Did Feller set a new record? Apparently he did, but *whoa!* Researchers at the weekly *Sporting News,* led by editor Cliff Kachline, checked through all Philadelphia Athletics box scores of 1904 when Waddell pitched, and discovered that Rube actually fanned 349 batters. The 349 figure was duly recognized, relegating Feller's strikeout total to second place. (Subsequently, of course, Waddell's record was broken, first by Sandy Koufax with 382 Ks in 1965, and then by Nolan Ryan with 383 Ks in 1973.)

Kachline commented on this strange statistical phenomenon: "Official scorers over the years turned in scoresheets with mistakes in them, often simple mistakes like addition. Researchers have gone over these erroneous scoresheets and made the necessary corrections. Thus, the stat has to be changed. Scorers erred because they were usually under deadline pressure. For example, newspapers wanted them in a hurry so they could be printed in a particular edition."

Kachline also mused, "Sometimes, the official scorers, who were working sportswriters, did not always show up to the game in any kind of condition to do accurate work. No wonder so many mistakes were made."

GREAT PITCHERS

THE QUESTION OF WALTER JOHNSON'S VICTORY TOTAL

When fireballing right-hander Walter Johnson retired following the 1927 season after spending 21 years with the Washington Senators, his victory total was given at 413 against 279 losses. Only Cy Young, who won 511 games, has a higher big league victory total than Johnson.

Strangely enough, however, Walter "Big Train" Johnson hadn't finished winning ballgames. Several years after his death in 1946, a number of researchers checked all of the box scores of games in which Johnson pitched and discovered that the scorers did not give him credit for three additional victories. Now all the standard references give Johnson 416 total wins.

Johnson's grandson, Henry W. Thomas, wrote an excellent and well-received biography on the "Big Train" in 1996, appropriately titled *Walter Johnson: Baseball's Big Train,* and said with great family pride, "My granddad was such a great pitcher that he won three Major Leagues games after he died."

Thomas added that the "Big Train" also struck out 11 batters after his passing since his K total was revised from 3497 to 3508.

Walter Johnson was reputed to have thrown a baseball as fast or faster than any other pitcher in baseball history. He was called "Big Train" because it was said that his best pitch traveled faster than any locomotive in existence. Radar guns were not invented during Johnson's era, but most baseball experts who saw "Big Train" in action said they've never seen a pitcher who could match his speed. In today's terms, his fastball traveled a tad over 100 miles per hour. No human could match that kind of speed.

In his 458-page tome on his grandfather, Henry Thomas repeatedly emphasized again that Walter Johnson made it a practice never to throw close inside to a batter. With his speed, Johnson, one of the true gentlemen of the game, never wanted to hit a batter with his blazing fastball.

Henry Thomas wrote, "If Granddad had pitched tight like so many pitchers of today — including Don Drysdale, who pitched in tight continuously — he could have become a 500-game winner. He never wanted to take a chance of hitting a batter with all that speed. If Walter Johnson threw inside as a matter of strategy, batters would be afraid to dig in. He gave the batters an even chance by not intimidating them, and he still established himself as one of the greatest pitchers of all time."

Two other stats reflect the true greatness of Johnson as a moundsman: his ERA stands at a very skinny 2.17 (good for seventh best on the all-time list), and he threw 110 shutouts, and that is *the record*. He threw only one no-hitter on July 1, 1920, against the Boston Red Sox.

EXTRAORDINARY MOUND FEATS
BY EXTRAORDINARY PITCHERS

Nowadays most big league pitchers "baby" their arms. In the old days, most Major League teams utilized a four-man rotation; now it's a five-man rotation. That is, hurlers today work every fifth day instead of every fourth day. And these five starters are backed up by a "relief crew" of seven additional pitchers.

The seven relievers are classed into categories: "long men," "set-up men," and "closers." Oftentimes, a reliever will be thrown into the fracas with the purpose of blowing out only a single batter. That "specialist" may be a left-hander whose job it is to get out a left-handed batter in a critical situation late in the game.

Today, moundsmen are taken out of a game if their "pitch count" reaches a certain number of pitches. Some starters are limited to as few as 100 pitches before they're taken out of a game. Very seldom is a starter allowed to hurl as many as 130 pitches per game. A relief pitcher, who often is called upon to "put out fires" two or three times a week, is limited to 30 or perhaps 40 pitches at most. The closer usually comes in to shut down the other side for a single inning. That is true of famous closers like Dennis Eckersley and John Franco. When they go past one inning in a closer situation they make news.

Strangely, there are now cases where a moundsman appears in about as many games as innings pitched. Take the case of Eckersley, one of the premier relievers of the 1990s: In 1993 with the Oakland Athletics, he appeared in 64 games and chalked up only 67 innings pitched; he did have 36 saves — a very good performance. Then with Oakland in 1995, he appeared in 52 games and hurled only 53 innings. He recorded 36 saves, and though his won-lost record was a less-than-mediocre 1-5, that stat doesn't mean all that much. Relievers are paid according to games saved.

John Franco's stats in respect to games played and innings pitched are similar to Eckersley's. While with the New York Mets in 1991, he appeared in 52 games and threw in $55\frac{1}{3}$ innings to go with 30 saves; in 1996 with the Mets, he got into 51 games and threw 54 innings, with 28 saves. Franco is the prototypical closer who rarely goes beyond a one-inning stint. Thus, complete games have become a relative rarity in the big leagues.

Greg Maddux, the star Atlanta Braves right-hander, led the National League in complete games in 1993, 1994 and 1995 with 8, 10, and 10, respectively — low numbers for the leader in that category.

Back in the old days, a reliever was often brought in with the idea that he would finish the game for the starter who was knocked out of the box. In general, lengthy relief appearances have almost gone the way of the carrier pigeon.

Eddie Rommel, the old Philadelphia Athletics star right-hander, spent the last couple seasons in his 13-year Major League career (1920-32) as a reliever, and he chalked up what is generally thought to be the longest relief assignment in big league history.

That came in a July 10, 1932 game against the Cleveland Indians. Athletics starter Lew Krausse was taken out of the game in the first inning when he gave up 3 runs and 4 hits. With two outs, Rommel came in to put out the fire. What finally happened was that this turned out to be one of the most unusual and highest-scoring games in Major League history. This wild and woolly games lasted for 18 innings before the Athletics won by a fat 18-17 score!

Strangely, Rommel was allowed to "go the distance," and he gained the victory with his "tight" relief pitching. In 17⅓ innings of work, he allowed 14 runs and 29 base hits. Clint Brown, the Indians' starting pitcher, was relieved in the late innings by Willis Hudlin and Wesley Ferrell. In this 18-inning marathon, the Indians stroked 33 base hits while the A's hit safely 25 times for the astounding total of 58.

John Burnett, the Indians' second baseman, established a record that still stands after 70 years: 9 base hits in a single game in 11 at bats. Indians' second baseman Billy Cissell had 4 hits, while first baseman Eddie Morgan hit safely 5 times.

For the A's, first baseman Jimmie Foxx picked up 6 hits in 9 at bats, while left fielder Al Simmons went 5 for 9. No doubt about it, the Indians and the A's had their hitting clothes on during that hot July day in 1932.

The Indians and Athletics were tied 15-15 after 15 innings, but both teams scored a brace of runs in the 16th to knot the score at 17-17. Then the A's scored a single run in the top of the 18th to put the game away at 18-17, a football-type score. Nowadays, a game of that length would require about six or so pitchers on each side, but in this monumental clash only five moundsmen saw action.

Rommel had a reputation for being a workhorse, since he had a string of games to his credit where he pitched well beyond nine innings. In an April 13, 1926, game against Washington, for example, he hooked up in a pitching duel with the great Walter Johnson. The Senators squeaked out a 1-0 victory over the Athletics in fifteen innings. Both pitchers went the distance, of course. That wouldn't happen today, because pitchers are rarely allowed to go beyond nine innings. Later on in his career, Rommel became an American League umpire and served for 23 seasons (1938–1960) as an AL arbiter.

We had the chance to speak with Eddie Rommel on several occasions. He was an imposing figure, standing about 6 foot 2 inches and weighing an athletic 200 pounds.

We asked Rommel why pitchers of his era were often able to work so many innings at a single stretch. He answered, "When I broke into pro baseball back in 1918 with the Newark Bears of the International League, we were just coming out of the 'dead ball' era and getting a new, juiced-up, lively ball that made it easier to hit homers. Even after the lively ball came into being in about 1919–20, a lot of hitters liked to continuing to 'slap' the ball and tried more than anything to 'place' relatively short hits. Ty Cobb was basically a slap hitter — I pitched to him many times, and he rarely tried to go for homers.

"Remember, Cobb became a little jealous of Babe Ruth hitting all those homers, and in 1925 Ty said, in effect, 'There's no real trick to hitting homers.' Then he set out to prove his point. In back-to-back games against the St. Louis Browns at Sportsman's Park early in May that year, Ty changed his batting style by taking a full swing. He hit three home runs in the first game, and two more on the following day, giving him five for the two games."

Historians indicated that Cobb was unlucky to hit seven homers in 2 days. Two of his shots missed the roof at Sportsmen's Park and dropped for doubles. Rommel went on to say that after that spectacular 2-day performance, Cobb went back to his old batting style, consisting of a snap swing and a quick chop so that he did not have to set himself. That made him able to shift quickly so he could meet any kind of pitch — high, low, inside, outside. The snap swing enabled him to meet the ball squarely even while he was shifting.

Rommel concluded his observations by saying that since pitchers in his era didn't have to worry all that much about game-breaking home runs, they didn't have to absolutely "bear down" on every pitch. He said, "We could pace ourselves." Rommel also emphasized that back in his playing days, pitchers objected to being relieved and strove to remain in the game as long as possible. Thus, starters of that era rolled up more innings per season generally than today's mounds-men. And by the same token, relievers didn't like being relieved, and that's one of the reasons he threw that famed 17⅓-inning, 29-hit relief performance on the afternoon of July 10, 1932.

BOB FELLER DIDN'T COUNT HIS PITCHES

From the time Bob "Rapid Robert" Feller broke in with the Indians in mid-season in 1936 as a 17-year-old who could heave the baseball 100 miles per hour, he was hailed as the Tribe's best pitcher since old Cy himself. When Feller enlisted in the navy on December 9, 1941 (2 days after Pearl Harbor), he had already won 107 games for Cleveland (against 54 losses). No pitcher in baseball history had piled up that many victories that quickly — not even Cy Young himself. Before Feller joined the U.S. Navy, many baseball historians thought that the fireballing right-hander had an even chance of at least approaching Cy Young's monu-mental victory total. However, Feller's navy duty took him away from baseball for 3½ years. He was discharged from the navy toward the end of July 1945. In his first game back, he defeated the Detroit Tigers 4-2 and struck out 12. He obviously regained his old form.

Feller went 5-3 for the last couple of months in the '45 season, and then in 1946 he turned in an almost unbelievable iron-man performance as he rolled up a 26-15 record for the sixth-place Indians. The Indians posted a mediocre 68-86 record that season; thus, Feller won nearly 40% of the team's games.

In 48 games, he pitched an almost incredible 371 innings, gave up a sparing 277 base hits, and came up with a skinny ERA of 2.18. He made 42 starts and led the league in complete games with an amazing 36. He struck out 348 batters, a figure that was thought to be a record, but later Rube Waddell's strikeout total with the 1904 Philadelphia Athletics was raised to 349.

Feller was thrown into relief situations six times so that he could pitch extra innings in order to have a better chance at breaking Rube Waddell's one-season strikeout record. No starting pitcher in the current era of baseball was ever called upon to go into a game as a reliever.

Still, Feller's regular season stats give only a part of his over strenuous pitching activities in 1946. Feller wanted to recover the lost baseball income during the nearly four years he served in the U.S. Navy. He organized a 30-day nationwide barnstorming tour composed of two teams consisting of Major Leaguers, plus top players from the Negro professional leagues. During that barnstorming tour, Feller pitched at least 60-70 innings in competition, and thus for the whole of 1946, he threw something like 450 innings. And that's not to say how many innings he threw in spring training in 1946. Nowadays no pitcher would follow a schedule that outrageously arduous.

Bob Feller would have piled up even more impressive lifetime pitching stats had it not been for a strange accident that occurred in a game he was pitching against the Philadelphia Athletics in June 1947. He fell off the mound — it was a bit slippery since it had been raining that day — and injured his right pitching shoulder.

From that point on, Rapid Robert was never quite the same again. He would never be able to throw those 100-plus mile-per-hour fastballs. But, despite the injury, Bob had a lot of baseball savvy and retained enough good stuff to remain in the majors for another decade. He finished the '47 season at 20-11, and then struggled through the Indians' 1948 pennant with a 19-15 record. While he led the league in strikeouts with 164 in 280 innings, that was well under par for Rapid Robert.

Feller's great ambition was to win a World Series game, but he failed in that quest because of one of the strangest plays in the history of the "Fall Classic." Bob started Game 1 against the Boston Braves at

Boston. The game was scoreless through the first 7 innings. Then, in the bottom of the eighth, Bill Salkeld singled to open the inning and Braves manager Billy Southworth sent Phil Masi in to run for him. Mike McCormick sacrificed and Eddie Stanky drew an intentional walk. Feller then attempted to pick off Masi, who had taken a big lead off second. Feller whirled around and fired a bullet to shortstop-manager Lou Boudreau, who cut in behind the runner. Masi slid back and was called safe by base umpire Bill Stewart, although Boudreau protested vehemently that he had made the tag well before the runner had reached the bag. Pitcher Johnny Sain then flied out, but Tommy Holmes came through with a single, driving in Masi. That was the only run of the game as Boston won the 1-0 squeaker. Films of the play revealed that Boudreau had tagged Masi out before the latter had gotten within 2 or 3 feet of second base.

Feller told us in a 1997 interview, "That was a strange call, all right. Stewart made a mistake because he was not in position to see the tag out. That's the breaks of the game." Feller can be very philosophical about misadventures in baseball. In going the distance, Feller allowed only two hits, walked only three, and struck out two.

After Bill Stewart retired from the National League umpiring crew several years later, he began a new career as a Major League scout. And who hired him to that post? Why, none other than the Cleveland Indians. Strange.

In the '48 World Series, Feller got a second chance to win a Series game. In Game 5 at Cleveland Stadium, a clash that drew a standing-room-only crowd of 86,288 (then a record crowd for any big league game), Bob was sent to the showers in the same inning with only one man out. He gave up 7 runs on 10 hits, as the Tribe took an 11-5 drubbing. The Indians did take the Series 4 games to 2, with Rapid Robert being the team's only losing pitcher against the Braves.

Feller went 15-14 and 16-11 in the 1949 and 1950 season, respectively — not bad, but not approaching Rapid Robert's past greatness. In 1951, he enjoyed an extraordinary season as he posted a glittering 22-8 record. Many sportswriters were ready to write off Feller as a front-line pitcher at this point in his career, and though Feller's fastball was no longer in the 100-mile-per-hour zone, he made up for it in craftiness. He struck out only 111 batters in 250 innings of work, but he led the American League in wins and in winning percentage with a .733 posting. Even at that fairly late point in his career, Bob threw 16 complete games in 34 starts (more CGs than most league leaders achieve today), including a no-hitter against Detroit on July (the third no-hitter in his career).

Toward mid-season, Feller was involved in just about the strangest of all games in his 18 years as an Indian — a game against the Philadelphia Athletics. The Indians had their hitting clothes on in that clash, and they whomped A's pitchers for 21 runs. The Athletics were no pushovers in the hitting department that day either, as they scored 9 runs. Did Feller get any relief in that slugfest? Absolutely not! He went the distance in picking up the victory. Today, if Feller had been pitching, he would have been yanked after 5 or 6 innings, just enough to get credit for a win, and the members of the relief corps would have been called in to mop up.

In our 1997 interview with Bob, we asked him why he was permitted to remain on the mound for the entire game when he was getting shelled. He answered, "I asked our manager, Al Lopez, to keep me in the game for a solid purpose. I was experimenting with a couple of new pitches, and I wanted to throw them in game conditions, so it didn't make any difference if I allowed Philadelphia to score a few additional runs, for we had the game wrapped up from the get-go. I know that you can't get away with stuff like that today, but I was glad to work out those pitches in competition and that did help me a lot down the road. And I've got to give credit to Al Lopez who allowed me to work on those new pitches. And I'm glad to see that Al made it into the Hall of Fame as a manager." Bob concluded, "I must have thrown at least 175 pitches in that game, but then nobody was counting."

Feller dropped to a 9-13 record in 1952, went 10-7 in 1953, and then roared back in 1954 where he posted a 13-3 winning season as a "spot starter." In 19 starts, he threw 9 CGs — not bad. That was the year when the Indians established a Major League record for most victories in a season — 111 wins against 43 losses.

Feller thought he had another shot at winning his first World Series game against the New York Giants, who finished the season at a comparatively modest 98-59. Unfortunately, the Giants swept the Indians in four straight games with Bob Lemon, Early Wynn and Mike Garcia taking the losses (Lemon two of them). Manager Lopez had scheduled Feller to pitch the fifth game, but since there was no necessity for a fifth game, Bob never got to pitch in the Series. Feller, philosophical as ever, said, "Stranger and worser things have happened to me before and since. I'm not going to worry about things that I have little or no control over."

Feller wound up his career in the 1955 and 1956 seasons as a spot starter and reliever, and in his 18 years in the majors he came up with a lifetime record of 266 victories and 162 defeats. Through the late 1960s, his strikeout total of 2581 ranked fourth on the all-time list.

While Feller may not have won a World Series game, he did participate in five All-Star games and went 1-0, having been the winning pitcher in the 1946 clash at Fenway Park when the American League clobbered the Nationals 12-0.

Bob Feller certainly wasn't through with baseball after he threw his last pitch for the Cleveland Indians. He continued to appear at old-timers' games and special exhibitions and kept hurling those balls toward the plate into the early 1990s, when he was past 70 years old — or "70 years young," to use our choice of words. Moreover, he still does his own yard work at his large home in Gates Mills, Ohio, near Cleveland.

DAVID WELLS— A SUPER BABE RUTH FAN

New York Yankees left-handed pitcher David Wells, who helped the Bronx Bombers take the 1998 American League pennant and the World Series crown with an 18-4 regular season record (including throwing a perfect game), has long been noted as a super Babe Ruth fan.

When Wells joined the Yankees in 1997, he asked to wear Babe's retired number 3. When that request was denied, he settled for number 33. From that point, he purchased one of Ruth's game-worn caps at auction for $35,000, and wore it in a 1998 game against the Cleveland Indians. Wells is known in baseball circles as a free spirit.

HALL OF FAMERS' SALARIES BEFORE THE AGE OF TELEVISION

Back in the so-called "good old days," most big league baseball players, even the biggest stars, hustled around to find temporary jobs in the off-season. During the 1940s and 1950s, many of the game's biggest stars, Hall of Famers, held everyday jobs. Duke Snider, Brooklyn Dodgers outfielder, carried mail from the Brooklyn post office during the holiday period; Stan Musial, St. Louis Cardinals outfielder/first baseman, worked as a clerk in his father-in-law's grocery store in Donora, Pennsylvania; Phil Rizzuto, New York Yankees shortstop, worked as a salesman in a New York men's clothing store; Mike Garcia, Cleveland Indians, worked in a Cleveland dry cleaning shop and then bought the business; Bob Feller, Cleveland Indians, sold insurance and then opened his own insurance company (which eventually went bankrupt); Early Wynn, Washington Senators, Chicago White Sox, and Cleveland Indians, was a construction laborer and then head of his own construction company in Alabama; and Carl Furillo, Brooklyn Dodgers, elevator repairman, Manhattan. We could list countless other stars who had to take on a variety of jobs following their playing careers, and those who had to work at odd jobs in the off-season in order to provide for their families.

It's been only within the past generation or so that baseball salaries have skyrocketed. Nowadays a player who signs a big multi-year contract is usually financially set for life.

We can state the reason for the almost geometric increase in baseball in one single word: television. Back when baseball games were first televised in the late 1940 and early 1950s, there were many baseball experts who maintained that TV would "kill" attendance at games. These so-called "experts" said, "Why would anyone go to a game if he could see it for free on TV?" It so happened that TV got many millions of new fans interested in the game, with box office receipts zooming as a result.

Back during the 1920s and 1930s when ballgames were broadcast on radio, revenues from that source were almost inconsequential. In many cases, Major League teams waived potential broadcast fees because they were happy just to get the free publicity.

The Cleveland Indians received their first "big" TV contract from station WXEL in 1951. That contract called for WXEL to broadcast all of the Indians' 77 home games, plus 6 games on the road. For those 83 games, the Indians received $250,000 — a lot of money in those days; in fact, enough money to cover more than half the player salaries.

Minimum salaries were not agreed upon until the late 1940s. When Jackie Robinson, the first African-American player in the Major Leagues, was promoted from the Montreal Royals of the International League in 1947 to the Brooklyn Dodgers under general manager Branch Rickey, he was given a $5,000 contract, the big-league minimum at the time. Player salaries before that time were generally paltry.

Then there's Jeff Heath, a Cleveland Indians outfielder from 1936 to 1945. He continuously complained about having to play for "peanuts." After he hit .343 and drove in 112 runs for Cleveland in 1938, he was given a contract for the 1939 campaign for about $3,000 — the equivalent of a Cleveland public school teacher's salary at the time.

After Heath finished his big league career with the Boston Braves in 1949, he signed a contract with the Pacific Coast League's Seattle Rainiers in 1950 worth $25,000 — the highest salary by far he had ever received in baseball. In fact, no minor-league player up to that point was given that type of generous contract.

Baseball salaries during the Depression era of the 1930s were generally very low, even for the biggest stars. Frank "Lefty" O'Doul led the National League in batting in 1932 while with the Brooklyn Dodgers. He averaged a fat .368. Did he get a raise for that performance? No. He was cut $1,000, down from $8,000 to $7,000, but he still ranked among the top-paid big leaguers.

Lou Boudreau, star shortstop of the Cleveland Indians, who as a brilliant sophomore in 1940 played in every one of the team's 155 games, averaged a solid .295, drove in 101 runs, and led American league shortstops with a .986 fielding percentage. For that grand effort Boudreau played under a contract calling for the munificent sum of $5,000, which amounted to little more than $30 per game.

Indians' owner Alva Bradley, a business tycoon with interests in myriad industries, felt guilty about that contract, so he gave Boudreau a $2,000 bonus at season's close. Then Bradley doubled Boudreau's salary to $10,000 — making him one of the higher-paid players in the big leagues.

MIKE PIAZZA AND THE TERMINAL TOWER

Sometimes the cost of player salaries becomes a little too steep, even for a multi-billionaire like Rupert Murdoch. Early in 1998, Mike Piazza, the Dodgers star catcher, demanded a 6-year contract, calling for a cool $100 million. Murdoch declined to offer such an obscene contract, and Piazza eventually wound up with the New York Mets before the '98 season got too far along. The Mets offered Piazza $85 million for six seasons, which added up to just over $14 million per year and would have been the richest baseball contract in history. Piazza felt he was justified in asking for a nine-figure contract because with the 1997 Dodgers he had perhaps the greatest hitting year of any catcher in the history of the game. In 152 games, he averaged a lofty .362, swatted 201 base hits, including 40 homers, and drove in 124.

However, the Dodger organization felt that Piazza, at age 30, would be vulnerable to injury as an everyday catcher, and that he might have a hard time fulfilling the extent of any overblown contract. Piazza was booed throughout the 1998 season by fans in most of the National League for his outrageous salary demands, but he took the jeering in stride as he rolled up another good year, batting .329 in 151 games, with 184 hits, 32 homers, and 111 runs batted in.

$100,000,000 is an enormous amount of money, especially when the sum is considered as a long-term contractual commitment to a baseball player. Consider Cleveland, Ohio, in connection with a massive downtown building project completed in 1930-31. The project featured the Terminal Tower (52 stories and 708 feet high, the second-tallest building in the U.S. outside of New York City), plus four other solid 20 plus-story structures, including the Midland Building. It cost a total of $ 100,000,000 — a massive amount of money in those days. Sure, the dollar is different today than it was two generations ago, but Mike Piazza demanding Terminal Tower money is zany!

GEORGE "SHOTGUN" SHUBA:
"I'D SETTLE FOR THE LICENSING FEE"

George "Shotgun" Shuba, who played for the Brooklyn Dodgers from 1948 to 1955 and who was the first National Leaguer to hit a pinch-hit homer in the World Series (in the '53 Series against the New York Yankees), discussed baseball salaries at length at a New York City card show. He said, "When I played, there were very few fringe benefits. Sure, some of the big stars, like Stan Musial, Yogi Berra, Ted Williams, Joe DiMaggio, and Bob Feller, made pretty fair money from commercial endorsements, but for the average player there weren't all that many opportunities to make money on the side. If I had the chance, I'd like to get a coaching job for a big league team, and I'd work for free. I'd just settle for the licensing fee."

The Major League Players' Association has an agreement with Major League Baseball to share all licensing fees for the use of the MLB logo as well as individual team logos on commercial products. The royalty fee is currently pegged at about 8%. Thus, if a manufacturer retails a jacket bearing the MLB logo, or a team logo, for $50, the MLB Players' pool will receive $4. Tens of millions of dollars of income are generated this way.

Currently, each Major League player, manager, and coach receives well over $100,000 in licensing fees annually. No wonder Shotgun Shuba would be willing to coach for zero salary!

HENRY AARON—
AUTOGRAPHS, YES.
REGISTRATION SIGNATURES, NO.

When anyone registers at a hotel or motel just about anyplace in the world, he must sign the registration book. But not Henry Aaron, the great home run slugger.

When Aaron appeared as an autograph guest at a show featuring all living Major Leaguers who had rapped out at least 3,000 base hits, an event staged at Atlantic City's Showboat Hotel and Casino in the fall of 1995, he flat out refused to sign the registry. "No way I'm going to sign that book!" Henry told the hotel clerk.

It seemed that Aaron's fee per autograph at the Showboat ranged from about $50 to more than $100, depending upon the nature of the item to be signed. (Autographed bats are the most expensive.) Henry Aaron simply wasn't going to sign anything for free.

The matter was settled when Aaron's agent signed the registry for him.

DIMAGGIO'S BIG BUCKS
FOR SIGNING BASEBALL BATS

While Joseph Paul DiMaggio refused to sign baseball bats at card shows, he did autograph lumber under special circumstances — and if the price was right. And DiMag's rates for bat signings were not cheap. There's something special about having a big star of the game sign a bat, especially one in the rare upper echelons in the Hall of Fame like Joe DiMaggio.

Of all of his deeds on the diamond, DiMaggio is perhaps best known for his 56-game hitting streak in 1941. Most baseball historians feel that this is one of the records that will not be broken. (Standing in second place for a consecutive hitting streak is Pete Rose, who batted safely in 44 straight games while with Cincinnati in 1978 — that's the National League record.)

DiMaggio signed bats for free for fans earlier in his playing days, but he stopped that altogether when the autograph craze started taking off in early 1980s. Sometime toward the end of 1990, an ambitious promoter asked DiMaggio if he would sign 1,941 bats to commemorate the 50th anniversary of his 1941 hitting streak. The promoter made DiMaggio an offer he could not refuse. He would pay the old Yankee Clipper exactly $2,000 for each signed bat. The promoter then proceeded to advertise the bats at $3,995 each!

DiMaggio, working in a private office, spent nearly 3 full days signing those 1,941 bats. For those labors, his check came out to a little under $3.9 million. No sports person in the history of this planet has made more than $3.9 million for less than 3 days work.

For a weekend card show, DiMaggio often cleared more than $100,000. In some cases, the promoter would take not a penny from that amount. He'd use DiMaggio as a "loss leader." The number of fans jamming into the place because of Joltin' Joe's presence would attract more business.

In the few years before his death, Joe was bringing in his own attorney to monitor these shows because he didn't want to miscount the number of autographs he signed. Remember, there was big money involved. Whenever there was a Joe D signing session, there was a big business atmosphere that breathed the "Fortune 500."

DiMaggio was also a stickler for "expenses" incurred while starring as an autograph guest at card shows. In a late 1990s card show appearance, he tacked on a $6.00 charge for taxi fare. We've got to watch those nickels!

Please don't misunderstand us — we fully appreciate Joe

DiMaggio's contribution to the game of baseball and to American folklore. We interviewed this baseball great on numerous occasions and he was always a gentleman. In fact, we consider ourselves lucky because Joe didn't ordinarily grant interviews to reporters. And he was always more than happy to give us a free autograph, which we gave out to friends. Thus, we established a personal relationship with him and stand in awe of his accomplishments.

DiMaggio's strange hold upon the American sporting public was dramatically illustrated at a mid 1990s card show appearance he made at Hofstra University. The show was staged at Hofstra's cavernous Fitness Center on an early Saturday afternoon, with over 1,000 people present, plus some 75 dealers, and several ex-star players' autograph guests. As Joe entered the room, a sudden hush fell over the crowd as all eyes strained to get a glimpse of the former Yankee great, then past 80 with a shock of pure white hair. DiMaggio, slightly stooped and with a history of medical problems, still maintained the majestic stride of a super athlete. Fathers lifted their small sons onto their shoulders so they could get a quick look at a true baseball icon, a legend in every sense of the word. This scene was of such magnitude that it could never be forgotten.

DiMaggio always took his autograph appearance very seriously. He dressed impeccably — a tailored suit, tailored shirt and silk tie. And even as he passed his 80th birthday, his signature remained clear and bold. He always took his time and signed carefully. Many big-time athletes just scrawl their signature at card shows.

At earlier card shows, DiMaggio would personalize any autograph, but starting in the early 1990s, he would sign his name only. At a full-fledged card show, he'd do 1,000 autographs on a Saturday, and then another 1,000 on Sunday; he just couldn't take the time to write out personalizations.

MARK MCGWIRE'S 70TH HOME RUN BALL SELLS FOR $3,005,000 AT AUCTION

The baseball hammered out by Mark McGwire on September 27, 1998, at Busch Stadium in St. Louis for his record-breaking 70th home run, brought an incredible $3,005,000 at a public auction staged a New York City's Madison Square Garden on January 12, 1999. The hammer price came to $2,700,000. With the auction house's commission, the total realization added up to $3,005,000.

It goes almost without saying that this marks the highest realization for any single item of baseball memorabilia sold at public auction. The winning bid was cast by Todd McFarlane, 37, a native of Calgary, Alberta, and now a resident of Tempe, Arizona. McFarlane, who claimed he spent his life's savings on this historic baseball, heads his own company, Todd McFarlane Productions, which produces a wide variety of comic books and related products. McFarlane, who is also a part-owner of the Edmonton Oilers in the National Hockey League, calls himself a "psycho baseball fan."

New official Major League baseballs, produced in a factory in Costa Rica, retail for about $6.

IT'S ALEXANDER CARTWRIGHT, NOT ABNER DOUBLEDAY, WHO INVENTED BASEBALL!

John Sterling and Michael Kay have been partners on Yankees radio broadcasts for a decade. Although we appreciate their general knowledge of the game and its wide array of intricacies, they have their zany moments on the radio.

Michael Kay once went into a soliloquy on the beauty and symmetry of the game during a Yankees broadcast early in the 1998 season. Toward the midpoint of the game, a player hit a grounder to deep short, with the shortstop coming up with the ball and throwing in time to the first baseman to get the out. Kay in effect said, "That's beautiful ... in the great majority of the cases, if an infielder handles the ball cleanly, his throw to first will get the batter out. The space between the bases, 90 feet apart, is just perfect. Thank you, General Doubleday, for inventing this great game."

The only problem with Kay's analysis is that General Abner Doubleday did not invent the game at Cooperstown, New York, in 1839, where the first ballgame was supposed to have been played. It has been proven that Doubleday (1819–1893) never set foot in Cooperstown and had nothing to do with the development of base-ball. Even historians at the Hall of Fame in Cooperstown agree, although Doubleday's mistaken connection with the diamond game is legendary.

Credit for the development of modern baseball, as we know the game, must go to Alexander Joy Cartwright (1820–1892), who orga-nized the first baseball team, the Knickerbocker Ball Club of New York City, in 1845. Cartwright's Knickerbockers played the first orga-nized game on June 19, 1846, at the Elysian Fields, Hoboken, New Jersey, against a club called the New Yorks.

It was Cartwright, an engineer and New York City volunteer fire-man, who set the basic rules of the game that stand today; including ending the practice of putting a man out by hitting him with a thrown ball. He introduced the nine-man team with an unalterable batting order, a nine-inning game, three outs per side, and a 90-foot baseline. He also dressed his team, made up of local firefighters, in the game's first uniforms. Most New York teams of that era came out of various firehouses. Barry Halper, the indefatigable New Jersey memorabilia collector, has a wide array of Cartwright materials, including his fire-man's hat and fireman's horn!

For his contributions to baseball, Alexander Cartwright was inducted into the Hall of Fame in 1938. Though there is a Doubleday exhibit in the Hall of Fame, Abner Doubleday was never elected into baseball's shrine.

The next time Michael Kay muses about the wonder of the 90-foot baselines, he should say instead, "Thank you, Mr. Cartwright."

CATCHING BASEBALLS THROWN OFF OF TALL BUILDINGS

Charles "Gabby" Street, who gained fame first as Walter Johnson's "personal catcher" with the Washington Senators and later as a pennant-winning manager of the St. Louis Cardinals in 1930-31, is destined to be best remembered for an offbeat stunt performed in the nation's capital on the morning of August 21, 1908.

Prompted by a bet between two local sportsmen, Street won a $500 prize and worldwide publicity by catching a baseball thrown by Johnson from the top of the 555-foot high Washington Monument. Though considerably jarred by the impact of the ball as it landed in his glove, it wasn't enough to keep him from catching Walter Johnson's 3-1 victory over the Detroit Tigers that afternoon. It was said that Street's experience on the receiving end of Johnson's "cannon-balls" had uniquely prepared him to accomplish the feat at the Washington Monument.

Several years later, Brooklyn Dodgers manager and former catcher

Wilbert Robinson was supposed to catch a baseball thrown from the top of a newly-built New York City skyscraper. Prankster Casey Stengel, a young Brooklyn outfielder, substituted a large grapefruit for a baseball. Robinson made the catch but he was furious when he found himself covered with grapefruit pulp.

In mid-season 1938, Cleveland Indians back-up catcher Hank Helf caught a ball thrown from near the top of the 708-foot Terminal Tower (then America's tallest skyscraper outside New York City). Helf made the catch, and today his name is still remembered for that performance.

Baseballs dropped from the height of skyscrapers travel more than 150 miles an hour when they reach the ground. That type of stunt has, for all intents and purposes, been banned by Major League Baseball as being too dangerous.

"SPLASHY" NEW BALLPARK INNOVATIONS

The Arizona Diamondbacks, based in Phoenix, became the National League's newest franchise in 1998 by going all out in making their new Diamondbacks Stadium one of the most innovative ballparks ever. Chief among the innovations is a swimming pool, together with an adjacent hot tub, beyond the outfield barriers. The pool area is housed in a special section of Diamondbacks Stadium. For a half-dozen seats or so, plus access to the pool and its accessories, fans pay more than $4,000 for season reservations. The fans can also catch some rays on a suntanning deck and, if they want, watch a little baseball.

The Tampa Bay Devil Rays, the American League's newest franchise, which also debuted in 1998, took second place to no one in ballpark innovations when they opened Tropicana Field. This way, fans who get bored with baseball can go down to a stadium super-mall underneath the outfield stands and shop for everything from shoes and shirts to new cars.

In the *Wall Street Journal* Sam Walker commented on the new era ballpark phenomena: Critics contend that all the sideshows won't build a true fan base and once the novelties wear off, some operators will lose money. Nevertheless, team owners see it differently; they say the added attraction will lure new groups to the stadiums and prompt them to stay, spend all day, and spend a little money.

ZANY BASEBALL CARDS: GLENN HUBBARD AND HIS PET PYTHON

In a 1998 survey, the weekly *Sports Collectors Digest* named the 1984 Fleer specimen showing Atlanta Braves second baseman Glenn Hubbard with his favorite pet, a 9-foot python, draped around his neck and shoulders, as the zaniest/wackiest baseball card. Hubbard seems to be enjoying the friendship of his reptilian friend, for he has a broad smile on his face. The python, a healthy-looking specimen, obviously has been well fed.

Baseball's Funniest People

STEER CRAZY

Home run slugger Ken Griffey of the Seattle Mariners and Team Manager Lou Piniella made a tasty little bet during batting practice in April of 1995. Griffey bet Piniella he could club a certain number of balls out of the stadium in practice. The loser of the home run wager would have to buy the winner an expensive steak dinner. Lou accepted the bet and the contest was on. Unfortunately for Griffey, he lost and had to pay up. Equally unfortunate for Piniella, superstar Griffey's unique sense of humor played a part in paying off the debt. Three days later, manager Lou Piniella walked into his office in the Mariners' clubhouse and discovered a 1,200-pound Hereford cow waiting for him. "There's your steak," Ken Griffey said to Lou Piniella.

OLD JOKE

Sometimes baseball players make honest replies to questions without realizing the humor in their responses. Take Hall-of-Famer Mel Ott, one of the game's greatest hitters. Young Mel was only sixteen years old when he was brought up to the Majors to play for the New York Giants. At the time, Ott was a catcher. New York's manager looked at the sixteen-year-old and asked him a question. "Son, did you ever play the outfield?" asked Manager John McGraw. Very seriously, Mel Ott replied, "Yes sir, when I was a kid."

HARE-BRAINED

Hall-of-Fame baseball star Walter James Vincent Maranville is better known by his funny nickname, "Rabbit." Rabbit Maranville played for the Boston Braves in the mid-1900s. Maranville was one of baseball's earliest pranksters. Once when it was his turn to bat, he crawled through umpire Hank O'Day's legs on his way to home plate — much to the delight of the hometown crowd!

HOMEWARD BOUND

Pitcher Pat Caraway of the Chicago White Sox pulled off a zany stunt in his rookie season in the Major Leagues. Caraway, who was a native Texan, found it tough to endure the bitter cold of early-season games played in blustery Chicago. He complained and complained and complained. Finally, the manager of the team, tired of hearing Pat grumble about the chilly weather, asked, "What do you want me to do about the weather?"

"Well," replied Caraway, "can I at least go home and get an overcoat?"

"Fine! Go get an overcoat," the manager shouted. And so Pat Caraway exited the stadium, left Chicago, and flew home to Texas to get an overcoat.

NAME GAME

After Mickey Rivers retired as a player, he got a job working with the New York Yankees and manager Billy Martin as a special assistant. One day during spring training, Rivers went into Martin's office and told him he wanted to be known from that day on as "Miguel Rivera" instead of Mickey Rivers.

"What's wrong with the name Mickey Rivers?" manager Martin wanted to know.

"Too many people are looking for me," zany Mickey Rivers replied very seriously.

THE HOLE STORY

In 1993, ex-Phillies infielder Dave Sveum was talking about his former team and said he missed playing in the City of Brotherly Love about as much as he missed having a hole in his head. When Philadelphia General Manager Lee Thomas heard about Sveum's comment, he fired off a fast retort that rates as one of baseball's funniest replies. "Dave Sveum is a real classy guy," he said. "We did give him an opportunity — a big opportunity. He says he misses playing here like a hole in the head. Well, what about the hole in his bat?"

SHORT STORY

Albie Pearson stood tall at the plate when it came to hitting, but he took a lot of kidding about his size. Someone once said of Albie, "If he walked around with a lit cigar in his mouth he'd burn everyone in the knee."

Another teammate of Albie's had this to say: "Having a catch with Albie Pearson is very relaxing. It's like throwing downhill."

NUTTY NEWS

Sportswriter Edward T. Murphy was a baseball fan with an ironic sense of humor. Trying to think positive during the 1930s, when the

Brooklyn Dodgers fielded some mighty weak squads, Murphy wrote, "Overconfidence may cost the Dodgers sixth place."

PIE-EYED

Larry Anderson was the team clown of the 1993 Philadelphia Phillies. Anderson, who liked to pester his teammates with wacky questions like "Why do people sing 'Take Me Out to the Ballgame' at the stadium when they're already there?" and "Why do people drive on the parkway and park in the driveway?" got a bitter taste of his own nutty medicine in April of 1993. While Anderson was taping an important television interview, teammates Curt Schilling and Pete Incaviglia sneaked up behind him and smacked him in the face with a shaving-cream pie. Larry Anderson's pie-in-the-eye television interview turned into an instant smash hit thanks to the practical joke.

HEY, IT'S BETTER WITH MY EYES OPEN!

INSIGHT

Paul Casanova, a catcher for the old Washington Senators during the 1960s, had a bad habit of dropping pop-ups. When someone asked him if he planned to make improvements in that area, he was ready with a witty reply. "This year I have a new strategy," Casanova said. "I am not going to close my eyes when I try to catch pop-ups."

LARRY "YOGI" BERRA

Hall-of-Famer Larry "Yogi" Berra, who played for the New York Yankees and managed the Yankees and the New York Mets, was not only one of the game's greatest hitting catchers, but also one of baseball's funniest guys. His wacky remarks, side-splitting stories, and nutty exploits are definitely of funny Hall-of-Fame caliber.

Food For Thought

When one of Yogi's favorite restaurants started to attract too many customers, Berra stopped patronizing it. When someone asked him about the restaurant, Yogi said, "Nobody goes there anymore. It's too crowded."

Eye Sore

Yogi was at spring training in Florida one summer when something weird happened during a rain delay. Two streakers jumped over the center-field fence and ran buck naked across the infield. When Berra went home that night, his wife asked him about the incident. "Were the streakers boys or girls?" she asked Yogi. "I don't know," he replied. "They had bags over their heads."

Home Boy

When Yogi Berra was the manager of the New York Yankees, he was interviewed at the start of the season. "I love home openers," Yogi said, "whether they're at home or on the road."

A Swinging Guy

In 1982, the New York Yankees managed by Yogi Berra had difficulty hitting home runs. In fact, during one stretch of 28 games the Yankee club clouted a total of only 14 home runs. Explaining his team's lack of power at the plate to the press, Yogi Berra said, "We're swinging at too many bad balls; that's why we're not hitting home runs." When a reporter on hand mentioned that Yogi himself was notorious for swinging at bad balls during his playing career, Yogi was quick to respond. "Yeah," snapped Berra, "but I hit 'em!"

YO! BROTHER

In 1934, Dizzy's brother Paul "Daffy" Dean was also a member of the St. Louis Cardinals pitching staff. In September of that year, the Dean brothers were scheduled to appear on the mound in a doubleheader against the Brooklyn Dodgers. Dizzy Dean pitched the first game of the doubleheader. Going into the eighth inning, Dizzy was hurling a no-hitter. However, in the last two innings Dizzy gave up three hits but still easily won the game.

Daffy Dean took the mound for the second game and turned in a dazzling pitching performance. He bested his brother's three-hitter by hurling a no-hitter for the win. After the second game ended, Dizzy ran out to congratulate Daffy. As the brothers shook hands, Dizzy asked, "Why didn't you tell me you were going to pitch a no-hitter? Then I would have pitched one too!"

A Bit Hit

One day the St. Louis Gas House Gang took on an opposing team that had a weak pitching staff. After four straight St. Louis players were issued walks, the starting pitcher was yanked from the game. The next pitcher walked two more Cardinals players and hit the next two batters with pitched balls. The ninth batter in the order, pitcher Dizzy Dean, then stepped up to the plate. Dean swung at the first pitch and dribbled the ball back to the mound. The opposing hurler had trouble fielding the ball and Diz was safe at first. "A fine team I'm playing on," said Dizzy to the first-base coach. "It isn't enough that I do the pitching, I have to do the hitting, too."

Weather Vain

While broadcasting on the radio a baseball game that was held up by a thunderstorm, Dizzy had this to say to his listeners: "If you don't know why the game is being delayed," said Dean, "stick your head out of an open window."

COLORFUL

Baseballs have always been white. If Charlie Finley had gotten his way, that would not be so. Charlie once tried to have the game of baseball played with orange balls. He even started a company that produced orange baseballs.

THOUGHTLESS—
THE LEGENDARY BABE HERMAN

Babe Herman was a great hitter for the old Brooklyn Dodgers. However, Babe resented the fact that he was sometimes referred to as a talented, but goofy, player. "I'm a smart fella," Babe once told a reporter. "I read a lot of books. Go ahead. Ask me a question about anything."

The reporter thought for a minute. Finally, he said to Babe, "What do you think of the Napoleonic Era?"

"Ha!" scoffed Babe Herman. "It should have been scored a hit!"

Ah, Skip It

Babe Herman's wacky ways are legendary. Babe didn't like to report to spring training, so he seldom signed his yearly contract until the season was about to begin. Everyone thought Babe "held out" each year just to squeeze more money out of the Dodgers team, which might not have been the whole truth. A teammate once asked Babe, "Is it worth skipping spring training every year just to get a few more dollars?"

Wacky Babe Herman, the worst fielder in baseball, replied, "I don't do it for the money. The longer I stay out of training camp the less chance I have of getting hit by a fly ball."

All Hail Babe Herman

The stories about Babe Herman's blunders in the outfield are endless. Babe was a terrible fielder, but such a terrific hitter that he was one of manager Wilbert Robinson's favorite players. In fact, in Wilbert's eyes Babe could do no wrong. That sometimes irked other Dodger players, including pitcher Hollis Thurston and backup catcher Paul Richards.

One afternoon, the Dodgers were beating the Chicago Cubs when Chicago pitcher Kiki Cuyler stepped to the plate. As Thurston and Richards watched from the Dodgers bullpen in right field, Cuyler swung and lofted an easy fly ball down the right-field foul line. The right fielder should have caught it . . . but the right fielder was Babe Herman! Babe never saw the ball. In fact, he never moved until the ball hit the turf just inside the foul line. By the time Babe threw the ball in, Cuyler was standing on third base with a lucky triple.

When the inning ended, Hollis Thurston said to Paul Richards, "Let's walk to the bench and hear what Robinson says to Herman about the fly ball." The men were sure Babe was going to get bawled out.

When manager Wilbert Robinson saw Thurston and Richards approaching, he stepped out of the dugout and scowled at them. "Hey, you two!" he hollered. "What were you doing in the bullpen, sleeping? Why didn't you yell to Babe that Cuyler's hit was going to be a fair ball?"

Triple Trouble

Could Babe Herman hit! However, he didn't always think straight. One day the daffy outfielder came to the plate with the bases loaded and no outs. He quickly walloped a triple. Unfortunately for Babe and the Dodgers, the triple turned into a double play when Herman raced past two of his Brooklyn teammates on the base paths in his rush to reach third base. The runners he passed were declared out.

Bonk

Babe Herman was a terrible fielder who muffed countless catches of fly balls in the outfield. Still, he always tried to convince reporters he wasn't that bad a fielder. "If a fly ball ever hits me on the head, I'll quit the game of baseball forever," Babe promised.

"What if one hits you on the shoulder?" a reporter asked Babe.

"The shoulder?" replied Babe Herman. "That doesn't count."

Bogus Babe

During his heyday, Babe Herman was a well-known celebrity. However, for a short period of time an imposter made the rounds of New York restaurants and nightclubs claiming to be Babe. "Look," Babe Herman said to the press when asked about the imposter. "Showing up that fake is easy. Just take the guy out and hit him a fly ball. If the bum catches it, you know it ain't the real Babe Herman!"

HERMAN "GERMANY" OR "DUTCH" SCHAEFER

Herman "Germany" Schaefer played Major League baseball from 1901 to 1918. He was a member of the Washington Senators, the Chicago Cubs, the Detroit Tigers and the Cleveland Indians. At the time of World War I, when Germany as a country wasn't too popular,

Herman Schaefer dropped his original nickname and called himself "Dutch" instead. No matter what name you call him, Germany Schaefer was one of the game's craziest clowns.

Hit or Be Missed

When Schaefer was playing second base for the Detroit Tigers, he entered the game as a pinch hitter. Since Germany wasn't known for his skill as a batter, the crowd booed. Schaefer turned toward the crowd and doffed his cap. "Ladies and gentlemen," he announced, "permit me to present Herman Schaefer, the world's greatest batsman. I will now demonstrate my hitting prowess."

Amazingly, Germany stepped up to the plate and clouted the next pitch for a home run. Germany raced down the line and slid into first base. He stood up and yelled, "At the quarter Schaefer leads by a head!" He then dashed toward second and slid into the base. He got up and shouted, "At the half, the great Herman Schaefer leads by a length." He ran and slid into third base. Germany jumped up. "Schaefer leads by a mile!" he yelled out as he ran for home. He slid into the plate and stood up. Germany Schaefer turned toward the crowd and made an announcement. "This concludes Herman Schaefer's afternoon performance," he bellowed. "The world's greatest batsman thanks you, one and all." He then trotted off the field.

FAMILY FUN

Someone asked catcher Joe Garagiola what Hall-of-Famer Stan Musial was really like. "Stan was a nice guy," Garagiola said. "Whenever I caught against him he'd step up to the plate and ask me about my family," Joe smiled and then continued, "But before I could answer he'd be on third base!"

Can't Resist

Sports broadcaster Joe Garagiola tells the story of Smead Jolley, a great fastball hitter. Jolley is up at the plate with runners on first and third. The guy on first breaks from the base to steal second. The catcher throws to second. The guy on third sees the throw and starts to run home. The shortstop cuts off the throw to second and fires a perfect strike to the plate. It's going to be a close play at home. At the plate, Smead Jolley watches intently. When the hard throw from the shortstop comes across the plate, Smead Jolley swings and cracks the ball into the outfield. "Hey," the home-plate ump yells to Jolley, "what are you doing?"

"Sorry, ump," answers Smead. "I couldn't resist. That's the first fastball I've seen in weeks."

Swan Song

Quick-witted commentator Joe Garagiola talks about a baseball team that was so bad that they had five runs scored against them during the National Anthem.

SAY, WHAT?

Frankie Frisch, the manager of the St. Louis Cardinals' famous Gas House Gang, knew how to have fun on the field. One day during a close contest, Frisch began to bug the home-plate umpire. Frankie complained to, yelled at, and badgered the ump inning after inning. However, the Cardinal skipper had enough sense not to do or say anything serious enough to get himself thrown out of the game. Finally, late in the game, Frisch shouted something to the ump from the St. Louis dugout. The umpire couldn't make out Frankie's remark. "What did you say, Frisch?" he yelled to the leader of the Gas House Gang.

"Hey," called Frankie Frisch, "you guessed at everything else today. See if you can guess what I just said." Frisch and his players roared in laughter.

"Okay, I will," shouted back the ump. "And for saying it you're out of the game, Frisch!" On the way to the locker room, Frankie Frisch didn't find anything humorous about the umpire's funny reply.

BUTT OUT

Umpire Frank Umont also had some hot exchanges with Earl Weaver. In 1969, Umont ejected the Baltimore skipper for smoking a cigar in the dugout before a game. The next day, Earl Weaver brought the team's lineup card to Frank Umont at home plate — with a candy cigarette dangling from his lips!

POOR GUYS

Texas Rangers outfielder Pete Incaviglia tried to make people believe Major League baseball players were not overpaid when he made this funny remark in 1990: "People think we make three or four million dollars a year," said Incaviglia. "They don't realize most of us make only $500,000!"

STOP IT

Baseball funny man Bob Uecker owns up to the fact that he wasn't much of a hitter during his playing days. Uecker claims manager Gene Mauch once said to him, "Get a bat and stop this rally!"

CLOUDING THE ISSUE

Outfield slugger Jackie Jensen of the Boston Red Sox launched baseballs into the clouds in the 1950s, but liked to keep his feet on the ground. Jensen was so afraid of airplane travel that he refused to fly to his team's away games. In fact, Jackie was so afraid of flying that he retired from baseball. He returned to the big leagues only after a year of therapeutic hypnosis, which cured his problem.

SHAME ON YOU!

Shortstop Johnny Logan, of the old Milwaukee Braves, was asked to pick his number-one Major League ballplayer of all time. Logan, who had a habit of mangling the English language, replied, "Well, I guess I'd have to go with the immoral Babe Ruth."

SEE YA

Major League baseball umpires have been the target of many wise-cracks over the years. Players argue with them. Managers and coaches complain about their calls. Even the fans criticize the men in blue. Way back in 1942, Gladys Gooding, the stadium organist at Ebbets Field, the home of the Brooklyn Dodgers, got into the act. As the umpires walked out on the field one day, Gladys played "Three Blind Mice."

THE PUPPET MASTER

In 1995, outfielder Andy Van Slyke, then a member of the Philadelphia Phillies, had a slight disagreement with a team mascot. In the heat of the moment, Van Slyke hit the mascot Bert from the children's television show "Sesame Street." Van Slyke thought the incident was forgotten until he stepped to the plate for a game in

Pittsburgh a few days later. As soon as he appeared, the stadium organist began to play the popular "Sesame Street" theme as a gag.

DIFFERENT, BUT THE SAME

Casey Stengel was asked to compare second baseman Billy Martin of the New York Yankees to second baseman Nellie Fox of the Chicago White Sox. In his best Stengelese, Casey replied, "They're very much alike in a lot of similarities."

Mental Problem

Duke Snider, the great Dodger center fielder, loved to listen to Casey spout Stengelese. However, at one point it did cause him some concern. "I got to where I could understand Casey real well," said Snider. "That sort of worried me."

Three Tries

When Casey was the manager of the New York Mets, one of his players was Marvelous Marv Throneberry, a fan favorite who never became a great Major League player. However, the hapless Marv was almost as zany as Ol' Casey.

During the 1962 season, Throneberry came to the plate late in a game against the Chicago Cubs. There were two outs and the bases were loaded. When Marvelous Marv hit what appeared to be a game-winning triple, no one was more surprised or happier than Casey

Stengel. Casey jumped up and down, and clapped and cheered. He was so busy celebrating that he never noticed that Marvelous Marv missed first base in his haste to get to third. However, almost everyone else in the ballpark noticed Marv's mistake, including the Cubs.

When the Cubs' pitcher tossed the ball to first base, Throneberry was called out. Stengel shot out of the dugout in a rage. He stalked up to the umpire and began to dispute the call.

"Calm down, Casey," said the ump. "Not only did he miss first, he missed second, too."

Casey, who was never at a loss for words, quickly fired back, "Well, I know damn well he didn't miss third. He's standing on it!"

Fired Up

Casey Stengel wasn't the type of guy to take complaints lying down. When the New York Yankees traded hurler Mickey McDermott, McDermott complained that manager Stengel never gave him enough chances to pitch. When Stengel heard about Mickey's remark, he was quick to reply in kind. "I noticed whenever anyone gave Mickey McDermott enough chances to pitch," said Casey, "a lot of managers got fired."

Wild Pitch

The "old perfessor" once said this about fastball pitcher Rex Barney of the Dodgers, who had difficulty throwing strikes: "He has the power to throw the ball through a wall," said Casey, "but you couldn't be quite sure which building."

KNOCKED OUT

Leo Durocher was famous for staging lengthy disputes with umpires. However, umpire George Magerkurth once got the best of Lippy Leo. During the course of an important game, manager Durocher was constantly complaining about Magerkurth's calls. Finally, the ump had enough. "One more word out of you, Durocher, and you're out of the game," the umpire threatened. Since Leo didn't want to get thrown out, he shut up.

A short time later, one of Durocher's players was called out by Magerkurth on a close play at first. Leo raced out of the dugout. Without saying a word, he grabbed his chest and pretended to faint on the playing field right in front of the home-plate ump. Magerkurth bent over the motionless form of Leo the Lip and shouted, "The runner is still out. And you, Durocher, whether you're dead or alive, you're out of the game, too!"

BILL VEECK

Bill Veeck was the P.T. Barnum of Major League baseball. As the owner of the old St. Louis Browns and the president of the Chicago White Sox, Veeck pulled off some of the wildest and funniest stunts in baseball history.

Veeck's Files And UFOs

In 1959, the UFO craze was sweeping the country. People everywhere were concerned about alien spacecraft and invaders from Mars. In Chicago, Bill Veeck was running the Chicago White Sox and used the lure of space aliens to stage a wild publicity stunt. On the 1959 roster of the White Sox were Nellie Fox and Luis Aparicio, two of the smallest players in the Major Leagues at the time. Bill Veeck arranged for "Martians" to land at the ballpark to kidnap Fox and Aparicio before the start of a game.

THIS ONE LOOKS LIKE A POWER HITTER!

BATTY

Lefty Gomez was always a weak hitter at best. Nevertheless, he couldn't pass over a chance to talk about his prowess at the plate. He once said, "I tried to knock dirt out of my spikes with a bat the way the big hitters do, and I cracked myself in the ankle and broke a bone!"

Throwing The Bull

Late in his career, Lefty Gomez was traded to the Boston Braves, who were managed by Casey Stengel. "The trouble with you," Casey told Lefty, "is you're not throwing as hard as you used to."

"You're wrong," Gomez answered. "I'm throwing twice as hard, but the ball is only going half as fast."

MAD MAN

Al Hrabosky, who pitched for the Atlanta Braves in the 1980s, was often called the "Mad Hungarian"! Hrabosky earned his nickname by talking to himself during games and by stomping around the pitching mound like a man possessed.

IN REVERSE

Zany! That is the only way to describe Jimmy Piersall. In his Major League playing days, Piersall pulled some really wacky stunts. Perhaps the best of his many gags was the way he celebrated hitting the 100th home run of his Major League career. It happened at the old Polo Grounds in 1963 when Jimmy was a member of the New York Mets. Piersall celebrated his four-sacker feat by running the bases while facing backwards. After Jimmy Piersall's nutty base-running exhibition, Major League baseball's rules committee outlawed backward base running.

HOT JOKE

One of former Major Leaguer Al Schacht's diamond tales deals with a conversation about baseball between Saint Peter and the Devil himself. The talk turned to who could field a better baseball team, and the two got into a heated debate. "Just remember," said St. Peter. "We've got guys like Babe Ruth, Lou Gehrig, and Roger Hornsby playing on our side."

The Devil nodded slyly. "True," he admitted. "But we've got all the umpires on our side."

ROYAL TREATMENT

When Dan Quisenberry was pitching for the Kansas City Royals, he watched in terror as his outfielders made a series of bad plays game after game. Finally, Quisenberry came up with a humorous suggestion for improving the Royals' outfield play. "Our fielders have to catch a lot of balls," said Quisenberry, "or at least deflect them so someone else can."

CAR SICK HUMOR

Satchel Paige never shied away from compliments or publicity, but a newspaper story about him once got him angry. The story appeared when Paige arrived in the Major Leagues in 1948. The article claimed that Satchel Paige owned a big, red car with the words "Satchel Paige, World's Greatest Pitcher" printed on its side.

"Now, that story isn't true," Satchel complained to his teammates. "I don't own a red car, it's maroon!"

MEAL TICKET

Cletus "Boots" Poffenberger spent most of his professional baseball career in the minor leagues. Nevertheless, Boots was one of the game's craziest characters. Once after he'd been called up from the minors to play for the Detroit Tigers, he checked into a fancy hotel. Poffenberger quickly dialed room service. "Send up the breakfast of champions," Boots said . . . and then clarified his statement by ordering six cold beers and a steak sandwich.

A STAR IS BORN

When Wes Ferrell was pitching for the Houston Astros in the Major Leagues, he was a student of the stars. Ferrell believed in astrology and always tried to get his starting assignments on the mound to coincide with his astrological "lucky days."

WRITE THIS DOWN

Pitcher Larry Anderson of the San Diego Padres provided lots of comic relief for his team. He was on the bench one day when he turned to a teammate and asked, "How do you know when your pen runs out of invisible ink?"

FUNNY FOLLOWING

Max Patkin played in the minor leagues as a pitcher, but is best known in baseball circles for his zany clowning on the diamond. He once served as a "clown" coach for Bill Veeck's Cleveland Indians team.

IF YOU LIKE MY PITCHING, YOU'LL LOVE MY CLOWN ACT!

Max's career as a diamond clown began by accident. Patkin was pitching in a service game in Honolulu against an Armed Forces team that included future Hall-of-Famer Joe DiMaggio. When DiMaggio clouted a homer, Max went crazy. He threw his glove down in disgust and stomped around the mound. Next, he twisted his cap so the brim faced sideways and contorted his face into wild expressions. As DiMaggio rounded the bases, Max Patkin took off after him. He followed Joe all the way home as the crowd laughed and applauded. And that's how Max Patkin's baseball clown act was born.

HEROIC FEET

Frank "Ping" Bodie was best known as the lonely roommate of New York Yankees star Babe Ruth. Babe spent so many nights out on the town that Ping once commented he "roomed with Babe Ruth's suitcase."

During a game in 1917, Bodie was thrown out by a wide margin while trying to steal a base. This prompted sports reporter Art Baer to write, "His heart was full of larceny, but his feet were honest."

You Make the Call

WALKS FROM THE PAST

The bases-loaded intentional walk is a rare case, but one such incident occured on July 23, 1944, when the Giants player-manager, Mel Ott, faced the Cubs and Bill Nicholson. The Cubs strongman had homered three times in the first game of the twinbill, and wound up with six homers in the series by the time Ott made his unusual move. Nicholson's hot streak pushed him by Ott for the league leadership for homers. All this set the stage, and in the second game of a doubleheader at the Polo Grounds, Ott, with a 10-7 lead in the eighth inning, gave Nicholson (who represented the go-abead run) a free pass with the bases loaded and two outs. Ott's logic was it's better to give up one run than four on a grand slam. For the record, the move worked, as the Giants held on to win, 12-10.

Legend has it that Hub Pruett walked Babe Ruth on purpose with the bases jammed on June 14, 1923, but reliable sources say this isn't true.

Nap Lajoie was actually the very first man to draw a bases loaded intentional walk. On May 23, 1901, the White Sox led the Athletics 11-7 in the ninth, but with the bases loaded and nobody out, player-manager Clark Griffith left the bench and became the relief pitcher. At that point he decided to give the walk to Lajoie, who represented the tying run. Lajoie would hit over .400 that year, but had the bat taken out of his hands on that occasion. The decision to walk him paid off when Griffith got the next three batters. So, while the move is extremely rare, it has been done. Still, don't hold your breath waiting for the next time a manager pulls this tactic out of his cobwebbed bag of tricks.

BACK TO OTT

Ott, by the way, was no stranger to drawing walks. He drew five walks in a game four times during his career — a record that still stands. He also shares a record for coaxing seven straight walks over a three-day period in 1943. Additionally, from 1936 through 1942, he compiled 100-plus bases on balls, also an all-time big league record.

Then there was the time he drew six walks in a doubleheader. He was playing against the Phillies on October 5, 1929, and, as the season was winding down, he was shooting for the home run title. Chuck Klein of the Phillies was also trying to win that crown. So, Klein's manager, Burt Shooton, instructed his pitchers to pitch around Ott. Klein, in part thanks to the Shooton strategy, went on to lead the league in homers.

OTHER FACTORS

Will Clark, the right-handed first baseman, was 6 feet, 2 inches tall and weighed 205 pounds. Dodger manager Tommy Lasorda knew he could walk Clark since first base was open. That would set up a force play at every base and allow the bullpen to face the number-five hitter instead of Clark.

Lasorda had already decided he was sticking with his reliever Tom Niedenfuer. The big (6 feet, 5 inches; 225 pounds) righty had entered the game when starter Orel Hershiser got in a tough spot after recording just one out in a 3-run 7th inning for the Cards. Niedenfuer was 7-9 out of the bullpen. He had 19 saves and an earned run average of 2.71 on the season.

Lasorda's dilemma was to issue a walk to Clark or to have Niedenfuer go right at Clark to secure the final out.

Keep in mind three final bits of information: First, Niedenfuer had absorbed the loss in the fifth game of the NLCS just two days earlier. In that game, he had surrendered a 9th-inning game-winning home run to Ozzie Smith, of all people. Smith was just starting to shed his "good glove, no stick" label in 1985, but even then he had hit just six regular-season homers.

Second, the Dodger reliever had already whiffed Clark to help calm down a St. Louis uprising in the 7th inning. If he had Clark's number, it might be best to defy common strategic practice and pitch to Clark.

Third, if the Dodgers gave Clark a walk, the next batter they'd have to face would be a lefty, the 24-year-old outfielder Andy Van Slyke, coming off a .259, 13 home run, 55 RBI season.

In such a situation, what would your call be?

The Actual Call And Results

Lasorda felt they could get Clark out. If your call was to walk Clark, you can gloat since Clark teed off on the very first pitch, jacking it out of the park for a pennant-winning home run. The Dodgers did have three outs left, but they were dead, going out one-two-three in the bottom of the ninth.

Incidentally, according to one version of this story, Lasorda instructed his reliever to pitch carefully to Clark, giving him an "unintentional-intentional walk." Still, a straightforward order for an intentional pass seems to have been the proper call.

While Lasorda's call took a lot of nerve, it also certainly went against the book. When you make such a call and things work out, you look like a genius. However, you wear the goat's horns when the call backfires.

TO HOLD OR NOT TO HOLD

Assume a runner is taking a lead off first base in a situation that seems to call for a stolen base. Also assume the runner does not possess the blazing speed of Brian Hunter, but he is a pretty good runner, definitely a threat to run, considering the game situation.

If your team is on defense, you might consider calling for a pitchout. You'd have the pitcher blister a high fastball way out of the strike zone, giving the catcher a ball he can handle easily. This strategy allows the catcher a great shot at gunning down the potential base burglar, especially since the pitchout gets the catcher out of his deep crouch.

Now, here's the question. Do you instruct your pitcher to hold the runner just a bit looser in such a situation? In other words, does the pitcher try not to tip off the runner that a play is on? In effect, does he encourage the man on first to run, almost enticing him, since you feel the catcher will fire the runner out. Is this wise?

Answer: Most managers would say you don't do anything special in this case. Rick Sutcliffe, winner of the Cy Young Award, once said, "You throw a normal pitch [a fastball with your normal delivery] to the plate. You glance at the runner with peripheral vision, but you do not hold him less closely."

According to Sutcliffe, the only thing that is different is that you don't throw over to the first baseman in an obvious attempt to hold the runner. So, you allow the runner his normal lead, but you make absolutely no pick-off moves when the pitchout is on. Pretty basic stuff, actually.

RUTH'S WORLD SERIES LARCENY

It's the 9th inning of the seventh game of the 1926 World Series. Today's winner will be the new world champion. The St. Louis Cardinals are leading the New York Yankees by a score of 3-2. You are the Yanks skipper, Miller Huggins, winner of 91 regular-season games.

Despite all that success, you are down to your last out. But all is not lost yet — Babe Ruth is on first base after drawing a walk. The game is still alive. If the "Bambino" could reach second base, he'd be in scoring position. A single could tie it up. Not only that, the batter now in the box is your cleanup hitter, Bob Meusel, and Lou Gehrig is on deck.

Meusel missed part of the season with a broken foot, but he still drove in 81 runs. Gehrig, meanwhile, had 83 extra base hits in 1926, his second full season in the majors. As for Ruth, he had swiped 11 bases during the season and was considered a pretty good base runner in his day.

Final Factors

The St. Louis pitcher was Grover Cleveland Alexander. Although he would come back in 1927 to post a stellar 21-10 record, the 39-year-old Alexander was on the downside of his career. He had pitched a complete-game victory just the day before our classic situation unfolded. Baseball lore states he had celebrated the win by going out on the town that evening . . . and into the morning. They say he didn't even witness the events prior to being called into the game because he was by then sleeping soundly in the bullpen.

Now, having worked flawlessly for 2 innings prior to the walk to Ruth, the game was on the line. He peered in to get the signal from his catcher, Bob O'Farrell, who had a .976 career fielding percentage.

Armed with all the data, what would you have done if you were in charge? Call for a hit-and-run play? Do nothing and let Meusel swing away? Have Meusel take a strike (not swing at a pitch until Alexander throws a strike)? This last would show whether Alexander was getting wild and/or tired; after all, he had just walked Ruth. Would you have Ruth steal to get into scoring position? Any other ideas?

What Happened

Ruth took his lead. Alexander fired a pitch, and Ruth, who had stolen a base the day before, took off for second. O'Farrell's throw beat Babe easily as St. Louis player-manager Rogers Hornsby applied the tag. The Series was over with the Yankees losing on a daring play that most experts felt was also a very foolish play.

Accounts of the game indicate that Huggins actually had Meusel hitting away and did not have Ruth running. The story goes that Ruth was running on his own, a terrible blunder. Few, if any, managers would have had Ruth running — it was way too risky.

DISTRACTION

At the Major League level, do managers and players employ tactics that work at the level of American Legion ball? Specifically, if you were a catcher, could you distract an opposing batter by pounding your mitt in an effort to trick him? The batter, hearing the sound coming from the mitt, can tell where the catcher is holding the glove. Presumably, he is telling the pitcher where he wants the pitch thrown.

The reality is that managers don't spend time teaching such tactics, but some players say you can distract or play mind games with your opponent. The story goes that one catcher used to toss dirt and pebbles into a batter's spikes to annoy him. Similarly, Yogi Berra was infamous for making small talk with a hitter in an effort to ruin his concentration. Remember when Hank Aaron responded to Berra's ploys by saying he was in the batter's box to hit, not chatter?

Mark Grace, an All-Star first baseman with the Chicago Cubs said, "Pounding the glove can work. It can distract you. It puts a thought in your mind. For example, the pitcher went inside with the last pitch, and the catcher is pounding the glove inside again. It can make you think. It's a mind game, but it doesn't stay in the mind too long." With a good hitter like Grace, once the pitch is on the way, such annoyances disappear, and the batter is set to hit.

Grace added that one thing that works for sure and is quite distracting is sheer intimidation. "It works for a pitcher," he stated. "That's what chin music is all about. A Nolan Ryan or a Dwight Gooden throws tight and sends a message: 'Don't dig in!'"

WHERE DO YOU BAT HIM?

Imagine you're at the helm of a pennant-winning team, and you're about to play the fourth game of the World Series. Would you consider batting your starting pitcher somewhere other than the traditional number-nine slot in the lineup?

Answer: You might, if the pitcher were George Herman Ruth. Babe Ruth left the ranks of pitchers after 1919, although he did pitch in five scattered contests after that. He became a pretty fair hitter, with a .342 lifetime batting average and 714 homers.

Actually, he was a fine hitter even while pitching — why do you suppose his manager moved him to the outfield full-time? In the last two seasons in which he spent a significant time on the mound (1918 and 1919) he was used as an outfielder in 59 and 111 games respectively. He hit 11 homers in 1918, then 29 the following year. Both totals were good enough to lead the American League. He also drove in 66 runs, followed by 114 runs.

So, with all that in mind, it's not so shocking to learn that in 1918 (his 11-homer year), in his final Series outing as a pitcher, he hit in the sixth spot for the Boston Red Sox. This marked the only time in World Series history that a starting hurler appeared any place but ninth in the batting order.

The Outcome

The Sox skipper, Ed Barrow, made a good call. Although Ruth grounded out early in the game, he tripled-in two of Boston's three runs. In his final at bat, he sacrificed. Meanwhile, the man who did hit in the ninth spot was a catcher by the name of Sam Agnew. He went 0 for 2 after hitting .166 on the year.

On the mound, Ruth worked 8 innings, got in trouble in the ninth, was relieved, then moved to the outfield as the Sox held on to win, 3-2. Boston also went on to win the Series 4 games to 2. By the way, during this game, Ruth's streak of 29⅔ consecutive scoreless innings (a record at the time) came to an end.

QUICK QUIZ

Do managers normally try to steal home in a situation like this? The runner on third can be anyone you choose. If you'd like, select Ty Cobb, who stole home an all-time record 50 times during his illustrious career. (Who wouldn't like that prospect?)

Now, does it matter if the batter is a lefty or righty as long as you have the fiery Cobb barreling down the line as soon as the pitcher commits to throwing the ball to the plate?

Answer: Yes, it matters. Most managers feel they'd definitely prefer a right-handed batter in the box when they attempt a steal of home. Back in the 1940s, Jackie Robinson was known to have done it with a lefty in the batter's box, but he was special.

Incidentally, stealing home was rather common in the Cobb era, a dead-ball era in which you'd scratch for runs any way you could come by them.

Lately, swiping home is a rarity. Wade Boggs, a sure future Hall of Famer, says that nowadays you just don't see it done. "It's probably a lost art. Mostly it's done now with first and third. The guy on first takes off, then the guy on third takes off."

Nevertheless, when an attempt to steal home does occur, you still don't want a lefty at bat. A left-hander stands in the batter's box to the right of the catcher. Conversely, a right-handed hitter stands on the left side of the catcher.

What's the logic involved here? Kevin Stocker of the Tampa Bay Devil Rays explained, "If you're on the right side of the plate, and you're straight stealing, the catcher can see the runner coming and has no one to go around." In other words, there's nothing obstructing his tag.

Or, as Atlanta Braves manager Bobby Cox, perennial winner of division titles, put it, "You want the batter in the right hander's box to help block out the catcher." A righty obstructs the catcher's view of the runner dashing down the line. The catcher may not realize a play is on until it is too late to do anything about it.

There was once a runner who stole home standing up. This happened because the pitcher threw a pitch that was so wild, the catcher was only able to grab it after lunging out of the line of action. Thus, he couldn't even come close to tagging the runner.

WHEN A CATCH IS OR ISN'T A CATCH

In 1991, Triple-A minor leaguer Rodney McCray was roaming the out-field for Louisville. On a long smash, McCray actually ran through a panel of the right-field fence near the 369-foot marker. David Justice called this the most amazing thing he had ever seen on a diamond. Justice was in awe of McCray's courage. "At some point he had to know that he had been running for quite a long time." Bone-jarring impact was inevitable.

Clearly McCray made a spectacular catch, hauling the ball in on the dead run under those circumstances. Or did he make the catch?

What's the ruling on this play? Is it illegal because he caught the ball but left the field of play because of his momentum?

The rule book states that, in order for a play to be a catch, the fielder has to have complete possession of the ball. In addition, the release of the ball must be voluntary, as opposed to, say, dropping the ball. Had McCray dropped the ball as a result of his impact with the fence, it would not have been a catch. As it was, the catch counted, and McCray became an instant hit on highlight films.

GREAT CATCH

A similar play took place on May 3, 1998, in Three Rivers Stadium in Pittsburgh. Turner Ward of the Pirates puffed a "McCray" when he crashed through the right-field wall after making his superb catch. Ward, who hurt his arm on the play, came back through the wall like a pro wrestler dramatically entering the ring. Then he short-armed the ball to a teammate.

SACRIFICIAL PLAYERS

Imagine that Bernie Williams of the Yankees is at the plate with a runner on third and nobody out. Williams powers the ball to deep left field where Barry Bonds races for the catch. Realizing the runner from third will easily score on the sacrifice fly, Bonds lets the ball hit his glove, but instead of securing the catch, he begins to bobble the ball. In a weird sort of juggling act, he continues to bounce the ball in and out of his glove while running towards the plate.

When he finally gets to very shallow left field, nearing the shortstop position, he lets the ball settle into his glove. The runner from third knows he can't tag up now, and he stays at third.

Is the Bonds trick legal?

What Bonds did will count as a legal catch. The runner from third, though, was foolish. The rules say you can tag up the moment the ball touches the fielder's glove, not when it is actually caught. If this play really had happened, both the runner and third-base coach would have been ripped by the manager and the media as well.

QUICK QUIZ

Here are umpiring situations that come up from time to time. You make the quick calls on these relatively simple situations.

1. A ball is rolling in foul territory between home plate and first base. Before a fielder touches it, the ball hits a pebble and rolls back into fair ground where it comes to a stop.

   Fair or foul?

2. Roberto Alomar hits a Baltimore chop; the ball hits home plate before it takes its first high hop. He beats the play out at first.

   Is this a single or a foul ball for hitting the plate?

3. A grounder trickles through the right side of the infield, just inside the first base line. It barely eludes Will Clark of the Texas Rangers. In frustration Clark turns, takes off his mitt, and fires the glove at the ball. The mitt strikes the glove, causing it to roll foul near the right-field stands.

   Make your call.

would have been two bases.
three bases. If Clark's mitt had struck a thrown ball, the punishment
for the batter. Any runners on board at the time also are awarded
3. The penalty for hitting a fair ball with a thrown glove is three bases
Give Alomar a hit.
2. Contrary to what many fans believe, the plate is in fair territory.
play, avoiding a cheap single.
touch the ball before it can roll back into fair territory. This kills the
halt. On slow-moving balls in foul territory, fielders always hustle to
1. The ball is fair. The decision depends on where the ball comes to a

ANSWERS:

FOLLOW THE BOUNCING BALL

On May 26, 1993, as Texas was playing the Cleveland Indians, a long fly ball off the bat of Carlos Martinez headed towards Jose Canseco. The not-so-hot-with-the-glove Canseco caught up to the ball, but he didn't catch it. In fact, the ball actually hit him on the head before soaring over the right-field fence.

Was it a ground-rule double or a homer?

The umpires that day ruled correctly that it was a (highly embarrassing) home run.

MORE BOUNCES

Back in 1993, Damon Buford was in the Orioles batter's box facing pitcher Matt Young. A pitch to Buford hit the ground and bounced up towards the plate. Buford didn't care that it one-hopped its way to the strike zone; he swung and hit a comebacker to Young. When Young lobbed the ball to first, Buford was ruled out.

Did the umpire blow this call? Should it have been a dead ball and no pitch?

Answer: The call was correct. Herb Score, a 20-game winner in 1956, said he once "threw one up to the plate that bounced, and the batter swung and hit a home run." Even if a batter is hit by a pitch that hits the dirt first, it counts. Such a runner would be given first base.

LITTLE LEAGUE CALL

Kids and even some Little League umpires seem to foul up the next situation. Let's say a batter hits a grounder to shortstop. The hitter beats the play out by a half step. His momentum carries him several strides down the right-field line. He then makes a slow turn to his left, towards second base. The first baseman is still holding the ball. Seeing the runner make his little turn, the first baseman tags the runner, claiming that if you veer at all towards second base you are in effect running there, giving up your right to saunter safely back to first base.

Is the defensive player correct in his logic?

No. This is a common fallacy of baseball. It doesn't matter which way the runner turns when coming back to first base as described. The only time you can tag out the runner is when he turns to his left and makes an actual attempt to go to second.

THE WAITING GAME

With no runners on base, Angels fireballing reliever Troy Percival came into a game to face the Baltimore Orioles. Percival, in a less dramatic version of Al "The Mad Hungarian" Hrabosky, went behind the mound to gather his thoughts. The home-plate umpire timed Percival, said he violated a delay of game rule, and called an automatic ball on him.

Can this happen?

Yes. The rule states that with no men on base, a pitcher has just 20 seconds to deliver a pitch. Thus, the relief pitcher was behind in the count, 1 and 0, before even throwing a pitch.

The umpires probably invoked this little-known rule because Percival is notorious for such tactics. The Orioles manager, Ray Miller, said of the relief pitcher, "This guy warms up, nervous as hell, walks around the mound, says prayers, bows behind the mound, looks over the center-field fence, and everything else. They got tired of it and called ball one."

MORE DELAYS

Albert Belle, Baltimore's volatile former slugger is at the plate. Let's say he gets irate over a strike call you, the umpire, just made. He starts to jaw with you. After a few moments, you get fed up with the delay and tell Belle to get in the box and quit squawking.

What do you do if Belle refuses to obey your orders?

In this case, you would order the man on the mound to pitch the ball. As a punishment, you would call that pitch a strike even if it isn't in the strike zone. In addition, if the batter still refuses to step in and face the pitcher, every subsequent pitch is ruled a strike until the recalcitrant batter whiffs.

In real life, this happened to Frank Robinson after he argued about a called strike two. Moments later, the umpire called strike three, and the future Hall of Famer had lost the battle and the war.

WHEN A NON-PITCHER COMMITTED A BALK

In May of 1984, Jerry Remy was playing second base for the Boston Red Sox when he caused a balk. Not only that, he did it without even touching the ball!

Here is how it happened: Marty Castillo of the Detroit Tigers had just doubled. The Sox felt he had missed first base and were about to make an appeal play. Remy thought there was a chance that the Boston pitcher, lefty Bruce Hurst, would overthrow the ball. Since it never hurts to back up a play, Remy positioned himself behind first base in foul ground.

Although the appeal was denied, a strange play resulted. The Tigers requested a balk call because Remy's actions, they argued, violated Rule 4.02, which states that all players other than the catcher must be in fair territory when a ball is in play. The umpires agreed with the Tigers' contention and charged Hurst with a bizarre balk. That's a clear case of an almost innocent bystander being victimized. Ultimately though, according to the rules, Hurst must take the responsibility.

AN EASY HOMER

On July 1, 1997, the Astrodome was the site of yet another crazy play. The Houston Astros were playing the Cleveland Indians. Traditionally, these two teams wouldn't meet during the regular season because they are in different leagues. However, due to interleague play, they were squaring off.

Each park has its own ground rules, so players need to know the quirks of the ballpark. Not knowing such rules cost the Indians a home run. Manny Ramirez, often accused of having a short attention span, was in right field when a Tim Bogar bouncer rolled down the first base line. Ramirez saw the ball come to rest under the Houston bullpen bench, and he waved to an umpire that the ball was out of play.

The only problem was that the bench was, in fact, in play. First base umpire Charlie Reliford gestured that the ball was still alive. Ramirez's hesitation and lack of knowledge gave Bogar time to circle the bases with an easy inside-the-park home run.

The Last Pitch

SCREEN PLAY

Some tricky third basemen run their own version of a screen-play when a runner is at third in a sacrifice-fly situation. Knowing the runner must wait until he sees the outfielder snag the ball before he can tag up, a wily third baseman might purposely get his body in such a position as to block the view of the runner. If the runner can't see the exact moment of the catch, he'll be a second or so slower at leaving the base and, thus, a step or two slower reaching home.

RED HOT CHILI

In 1995, Sandy Alomar's backup catcher, Tony Pena, and Dennis Martinez recreated one of the most famous trick plays ever. The first time this bit of deception took place was during the 1972 World Series. The Oakland A's were in a situation in which an intentional walk to Johnny Bench made sense. They went through the motions, but at the last second they fired strike three past the befuddled Bench.

Actually, World Series-bound Cleveland did the A's one better — they got away with it on two occasions. Pena and Martinez cooked up the play on their own. Alomar recalled: "Dennis was struggling, and he needed a play to get out of an inning. He had thrown a lot of pitches, and it was a perfect situation to do it. It was a smart play. It worked on Chili Davis who was very upset about it. They did it one time to John Olerud."

It seems incredible that this play could work twice in a season in this day and age when highlights are constantly played and replayed on television. Alomar concurred, "If I'm a player for a different team, I guarantee you I see that on ESPN, and they wouldn't get me."

JETER APPROVES

The 1996 American League Rookie of the Year, Derek Jeter, was asked what trick plays he's seen that were interesting or unusual. Without skipping a beat, the Yankee shortstop responded, "Tony LaRussa batting the pitcher eighth over there in St. Louis — that's a little different!"

Arguments aside about whether or not this is actually a trick play, he's right. On July 9, 1998, when he penciled his starter in at the number-eight spot, LaRussa made Todd Stottlemyre the first big league pitcher in twenty years to bat anywhere but last in the order. Although Stottlemyre did hit .236 the previous season, there was another reason for the strategy. At first, some fans thought LaRussa was doing this because the man who did bat ninth, Placido Polanco, might be a weak hitter. Also, Polanco was making just his second major league start.

Fans and writers recalled that the last pitcher to hit higher than ninth was Philadelphia's Steve Carlton on June 1, 1979. In that case, it was true that Carlton was often a bigger threat with the bat than, say, Bud Harrelson, who hit ninth when Carlton was in the number-eight spot.

After much speculation, the truth came out. LaRussa revealed that his motive for the move was to get more men on base ahead of the heart of the lineup. Not a bad thought, especially when the aorta of that heart is big Mark McGwire, who was in the midst of chasing Roger Maris and the single-season home run record of 61.

Said the St. Louis manager, "I don't see how it doesn't make sense for the ninth-place hitter to be a legitimate hitter. This gives us a better shot to score runs. It's an extra guy on base in front of Ray Lankfort, Mark McGwire, and Brian Jordan. The more guys who are on base, the less they'll be able to pitch around Mark."

LaRussa said he first conceived of the scheme at the All-Star break and that it "doesn't have anything to do with the pitcher." Nothing, that is, except get his weak bat out of the way and allow a real hitter in the ninth spot to become, in effect, an additional leadoff hitter in front of McGwire and Company.

A logical question for LaRussa, then, was why not just drop McGwire to the cleanup position so he could always have three bona fide hitters preceding him. However, LaRussa said that because McGwire hits third, he come to the plate in the 1st inning of every game, a big advantage in LaRussa's book.

LAME TRICK

Many baseball fans feel the trick play in which the pitcher fakes a throw towards the runner off third base, then swivels, fire and tries to pick off the runner from first is lame. Somehow, though, it succeeded in 1998.

On the last day in June, the Oakland A's were hosting the San Diego Padres. Entering the top of the ninth, Oakland was clinging to a 12-8 lead. Two outs later, the Padres were rallying. They had scored two runs. Now they had a runner at third with the tying run on first.

With a 2-and-2 count on Mark Sweeney, A's catcher Mike Macfarlane gave reliever Mike Fetters the sign to put on a special pick-off move. Fetters, however, was confused — he had spent the last six years with the Milwaukee Brewers and momentarily mixed up their signals with those of the A's.

So Macfarlane waved his hand in the direction of first, then third to indicate what he wanted. Even after all of that blatant gesturing, Padres runner Ruben Rivera was caught snoozing. Eventually, the rookie Rivera was tagged out trying to make it to second base.

A's manager Art Howe was thinking along the lines of Tony Pena when he called his trick play. "It just didn't seem like anybody was going to make an out, so I said, 'Let's manufacture one,'" commented Howe.

The play was especially mortifying for several reasons. For example, it's foolish to do anything risky (or not pay attention) on the bases in such a situation. After all, this play ended the game and gave the A's a win. Not only that, Rivera was in the game for his running skills — the Padres had just put him in moments earlier as a pinch runner.

Oakland's Jason Giambi observed, "You know the old theory about that play never working? Well, it did today."

THE 300 CLUB

Certain numbers have a magical quality in baseball. For example, as a rule, if a hitter connects for 500 homers, he's headed for the Hall of Fame. For pitchers, making it into the 300-Win Club — a highly exclusive circle of stars — is a coveted goal. Has a pitcher ever managed to lose 300 games?

Answer: Yes, and ironically the man to lose the most games in big league history (313 to be precise) is the same man whose name graces the trophy that personifies pitching excellence — Cy Young. So the award given for pitching excellence actually has its origin with the game's biggest loser. Of course, to be fair, Young also won a staggering 511 games, the most ever in the annals of the game. The next highest win total is nearly 100 less than that — Walter Johnson's 416 victories.

By the way, the only other man to drop 300 decisions was an obscure pitcher from the late nineteenth century named Pud Galvin. This right-hander made it to the Hall of Fame, as did Young. Galvin pitched only 14 years, yet he won 361 games and had such unusual numbers as a 46-29 won-lost record in 1883 and 46-22 the next season.

Imagine, he won 92 games in just two years — that's four and a half to five years' worth of toil for a good pitcher today. Of course, his 51 losses over that two-year span would also take quite a few years for a good pitcher to reach today.

BETTER
THAN PERFECT

This question involves a very famous game that took place in the 1950s. Did a pitcher ever throw a perfect game that went beyond 9 innings?

Answer: Even though the above question seems to give away the answer, this question, like a Gaylord Perry pitch, is loaded. While it's true Harvey Haddix threw a perfect game that went into the 13th inning back in 1959, a bizarre ruling by baseball officials in 1991 took away his perfect game status. The rule states that in order for a pitcher to get credit for a no-hitter, he must pitch 9 innings and pitch the whole game (including the innings beyond the ninth) without surrendering a hit. Therefore, what most experts agree was the most perfect game ever is not recognized as such.

Here's what happened on that historic night. Haddix, a diminutive lefty for the Pirates, was perfect through 12 innings against the Milwaukee Braves. Felix Mantilla led off the 13th and reached base on a throwing error by Pirates third baseman Don Hoak. Eddie Mathews then sacrificed the runner to scoring position. That prompted

Pittsburgh manager Danny Murtaugh to issue an intentional walk to the dangerous Hank Aaron, setting up a double play.

Pandemonium ensued when Joe Adcock homered. But, due to yet another baseball rule, he only received credit for a double. The reason he was robbed of a home run isn't quite as bizarre as the ruling that hurt Haddix, however. Aaron saw the ball soaring deep and figured it would drop near the fence, so he touched second base, but he never bothered to go to third. As Adcock rounded the bags and touched third base, he was technically guilty of passing a runner and, therefore, received credit for two bases, not four. Adcock also received just one run batted-in instead of three.

MARTINEZ ALSO ROBBED

In 1995, Montreal Expos pitcher Pedro Martinez also got ripped off by the new no-hitter rule. Facing the Padres, he was perfect through 9 innings. Shortly thereafter, when Bip Roberts doubled to lead off the tenth, the perfect game was gone. Martinez then gave way to closer Mel Rojas, who retired the last three batters. The expos went on to win a 1-0 classic.

Roster